MMB MUSIC, INC.

CONTEMPORARY ARTS BUILDING
3526 WASHINGTON AVENUE
SAINT LOUIS, MISSOURI 63103-1019 USA
314 531-9635; 800 543-3771 (USA/Canada); Fax 314 531-8384
http://www.mmbmusic.com

Movement and Rhythmic Activities for the Mentally Retarded

MMB MUSIC, INC.

CONTEMPORARY ARTS BUILDING
3526 WASHINGTON AVENUE
SAINT LOUIS, MISSOURI 63103-1019 USA
314 531-9635; 800 543-3771 (USA/Canada); Fax 314 531-8384
http://www.mmbmusic.com

Movement and Rhythmic Activities for the Mentally Retarded

By

CYNTHIA D. CRAIN, M.A.

Dance Educator
Virginia Polytechnic Institute
and State University
Blacksburg, Virginia

CHARLES C THOMAS • PUBLISHER
Springfield • Illinois • U.S.A.

Published and Distributed Throughout the World by
CHARLES C THOMAS ● PUBLISHER
Bannerstone House
301-327 East Lawrence Avenue, Springfield, Illinois, U.S.A.

© *1981, by* CHARLES C THOMAS ● PUBLISHER
ISBN 0-398-04174-1
Library of Congress Catalog Card Number: 80-26129

. *Printed in the United States of America*
V-R-1

Library of Congress Cataloging in Publication Data
Crain, Cynthia D
   Movement and rhythmic activities for the men-
tally retarded.

   Bibliography:
   Includes index.
   1. Movement education. 2. Physical education
for mentally handicapped children. I. Title.
[DNLM: 1. Movement. 2. Motor activity.
3. Mental retardation--Rehabilitation. WM 300 C887m]
GV452.C7   371.9′044   80-26129
ISBN 0-398-04174-1

to Stacy

PREFACE

TEACHERS and recreators that I have been in contact with for the past ten years have often requested assistance or advice in the area of movement and rhythms. Although this area has become widely accepted and implemented in elementary physical education programs, the progress in special education has been slow but forthcoming. The problem with many attempted movement programs in special education is that they have been too difficult and lacked the foundation of basic skills. All too often I have witnessed the special educator or recreator attempting to start a movement and rhythms program for the first time by introducing entire folk or square dances. The end result has been the abandonment of such programming.

This manuscript is a guide for teachers, recreators, youth serving agency leaders, and others who would like a better understanding of movement and rhythms. From the beginning, the book introduces simple yet necessary basic movement terms and skills to prepare both the teachers and participants for more complex activities. Through orientation, exploration, dances, and rhythms the mentally retarded can improve bodily control and self-image.

Movement and rhythms is one part of the broad fine arts area that can provide a means of self-expression through nonverbal communication. The mentally retarded are members of society who have different needs from nonretarded members. The mentally retarded often have nothing but leisure hours to fill throughout the day. They may be delayed or handicapped in speech and therefore require other mediums for expression. Most importantly, they are people who need fulfillment and a knowledge of self-worth.

Movement and Rhythmic Activities for the Mentally Retarded is not a remedy or a cure. Instead, it provides pertinent information to guide the enthusiastic and venturesome person in his first attempt at providing a movement and rhythms program, challenges and offers new suggestions for the existing program, and organizes old terminology into a modified classification system based on a combined dance, choreography, and kinesiology perspective.

The handicapped can move; some can draw, act, sing, and dance. The success of a fine arts program is limited only to those in the leadership positions, not dancers, artists, musicians, and stage directors but classroom teachers, community recreators, and volunteers who seek challenges and creative programming through the arts.

CONTENTS

                                                              Page

: *Preface* vii

Chapter

1. INTRODUCTION 3
       Movement.. 4
       Rhythm.. 5
       Movement, Rhythm, and the Mentally Retarded....... 6
2. MOVEMENT ORIENTATION 8
       Movement Orientation Activities 8
           Perceptual Motor Activities 9
           Sensory Motor Activities......................... 10
           Balance Improvement Activities 11
           Muscular Integration Activities................... 15
           Tumbling Activities.............................. 18
           Physical Fitness Activities 24
       The Value of a Movement Orientation Program 29
3. MOVEMENT EXPLORATION 31
       Nonlocomotor Activities........................... 31
       Locomotor Activities 34
       Movement Components 37
       Movement Qualities............................... 38
       The Value of a Movement Exploration Program 40
4. DANCE.. 41
       Folk Dance....................................... 42
       Square Dance..................................... 44
       Modern Dance.................................... 47
           Modern Dance Nomenclature 48
       Creative Dance 54
       The Value of Dance 58

Chapter   *Page*

5. RHYTHM 60
      Action Songs 60
      Rhythm Instruments 62
      Parachute and Other Activities...................... 63
      Value of Rhythm 72
6. WORKING WITH THE MENTALLY RETARDED: HINTS AND
      SUGGESTIONS 73
      Teacher Objectives 74
      Pupil Objectives 75
      Activity Objectives 77
      Activity Selection 78
         Adapting Activities............................... 80
      Criteria for Program Assessment 80
7. SUGGESTED PROGRAM ACTIVITIES AND EQUIPMENT 82
      Warm-up... 82
      Spacial Orientation 83
      Physical Fitness.................................... 85
      Body Awareness 87
      Dance.. 88
      Relaxation 90
      Conclusion 91

Appendix
   A. Examples of Movement and Music Activity
      Lesson Plans for the Mentally Retarded 97
   B. Even and Uneven Rhythmic Patterns.................. 114
   Suggested Records 119
   Bibliography 121
   Index... 125

Movement and
Rhythmic Activities for
the Mentally Retarded

Chapter 1

INTRODUCTION

THE mentally retarded population, whether institutionalized or homebound, is a group that is capable of learning certain cognitive and physical skills as other persons can, but in varying degrees. Motor patterns and skills that are often taken for granted when a child is growing, e.g. the hop, skip, and run, may be nonexistent or develop into splinter skills, which will possibly impede increased development and proficiency of certain motor development on the part of the retarded person. This does not mean, however, that these skills and motor patterns cannot be taught and learned by the mentally retarded during their lifetime. Instead, it is necessary that an emphasis on specialized instruction in various kinds of motor development be provided as a fundamental part of the teaching/learning process for the mentally retarded.

In order to obtain the ascribed goals and objectives inherent in the teaching/learning process, it is important that programmed activities be planned that will enable the retardates to fulfill their individual ability potentials. Concurrently, there are certain needs that will also affect accomplishment, and therefore, objectives should be planned that will strive to fulfill these needs. Finally, to round off the total activities program, a proper working environment and rapport is necessary between the teacher and his students. The environment of the typical activity session will probably look like a play period to the casual observer rather than an education milieu. However, it is important to keep in mind that play is educational, and because the mentally retarded should be educated in a setting that is flexible, undemanding, and fun, an atmosphere that is centered around play type activities is ideal. This does not mean that structure, conformity, and/or problem-solving pedagogies will be precluded from these sessions; actually, they should comprise the premise on which purposes and objectives for each activity session is formulated. Instead, it is necessary to remember that control is essential in conducting the activities sessions but that rigidity is not.

A specific part of the total educational process that can provide one type of program for (1) teaching motor skills and patterns, (2) focusing on needs of the mentally retarded, and (3) conjuring an environment that is recreational is found in the movement and rhythmic activities program.

Movement and rhythm have been established as valid and vital parts of any educational activity program concerning the mentally retarded population (Cratty, 1969; Leventhal, 1974). Movement has been described as (1) a personality reflection (Kalish and Kestenbury, 1974); (2) a "useful tool in helping to relieve a child's anxiety, helping to focus the hyperactive child, and helping the minimal brain damaged child to establish a more positive self-concept" (Leventhal, 1974); and (3) a means of improving sensory attention and perceptual-motor coordination (Godfrey and Kephart, 1969; Cratty, 1969; Leventhal, 1974).

Rhythm has been described as follows: (1) a means in which the probability that movement accomplishments will result is increased, (2) a help in facilitating movement activities, and (3) a means whereby body awareness is developed, both internally and externally. In addition, rhythm and movement are inseparable; it is movement that manipulates the drumstick in order to maintain a certain rhythm and tempo on the drum, and it is movement that articulates the legs and feet while marching.

MOVEMENT

Movement occurs when the total body or a body segment changes/alters a position in any way. Movement of the body is a means of experiencing and relating to one's world. During the movement experience a *bodily* awareness should be experienced. It is this body awareness with which movement experience and movement exploration are concerned. In order to determine whether or not you are physically aware of yourself (body awareness) ask yourself these questions: (1) what type of grip do you have when shaking hands — is it firm or weak; (2) at this time, where is your head positioned — is it tilted backward or forward, inclined to the right or left, turn to the right or left; and (3) if you are in a sitting position, without looking, can you detect which parts of your body are in touch with the chair or floor — the lower back, the back of the knees, the entire foot, the ball of the foot?

This is a simple exercise in body awareness, but it is helpful in heightening your senses (e.g. touch and kinesthetic awareness) and for detecting inappropriate body positioning that may be causing undue stress. The next time you are driving a car or sitting at a desk and you feel your neck beginning to ache or your head beginning to throb, if it is not induced by poor lighting or glare, check to see whether you have been contracting your upper shoulders, back, and/or neck muscles for a period of time. If you can lower your shoulders, which lengthens the neck, and relax, you will probably recognize that your body, through pain, was trying to make you aware of the strained position. This is only one example of heightening body awareness. Through increased body awareness one may learn (1) to recognize his own individual movement potential, (2) to realize his need for coordination and control of movement for everyday task accomplishments, and (3) to assess individually what his body is doing as a check for appropriate or inappropriate movement behavior.

RHYTHM

Rhythm has been defined by Jaques-Dalcroze (1930) as a movement series that form a whole (e.g. phrase) and is capable of being repeated. Within the general term rhythm, there are certain components: (1) tempo — how slow or fast, and (2) rhythmic structure or beat — even and uneven. Rhythm is the means of providing efficiency in movement, i.e. to obtain the maximum effect with a minimum of effort (Jaques-Dalcroze, 1930). Expiration/inhalation and the pulsating cardiac muscles of the viscera have a certain predisposed rhythm. The contrived use of a drum dictates a certain beat or rhythm. Therefore, rhythm may be involuntary or voluntary and perpetually exists until cessation or death. Rhythm also plays a functionally important role in the areas of physical fitness, sensory training, and creative expression.

MOVEMENT, RHYTHM, AND THE MENTALLY RETARDED

Movement and rhythm are inseparable when implemented in the activity program for the mentally retarded. Movement and rhythm are highly effective means in helping the retardate to develop socially, psychologically, and physically, even if this development is indirectly influenced. The following chapters are designed to provide the teacher of the mentally retarded with the basic knowledge and information concerning a movement and rhythmics activity program. In addition, the text hopes to establish a foundation of movement skills and patterns with which the teacher can become familiar so that there-will be less awkwardness and inhibition on the part of the teacher in attempting to use movement and rhythms in the activity program.

The second chapter, entitled "Movement Orientation," is designed to familiarize the teacher and the mentally retarded persons with activities that will render the participants more physically fit while developing body awareness through gross motor exercises that are simple and fun. Chapter 3, "Movement Exploration," deals with (1) exploring different ways of moving the body and (2) defining and experiencing what movement is. Activities are chosen that will help the mentally retarded understand movement through the manipulation of body parts in a variety of ways. Chapter 4, "Dance," depicts how movement orientation activities, movement exploration, and rhythmic activities can be combined, codified, and added to some form of musical accompaniment for broadening and enhancing the overall movement experience. Dance is extremely beneficial in working with the mentally retarded because of the opportunities provided for psychological, physical, and social development within a recreational milieu that is also positive and enjoyable. Chapter 5, "Rhythm," provides the teacher with examples of fundamental equipment/instruments and usage of the equipment. Rhythmic activities are a basic part of a movement activities program. Emphasis in developing selected rhythmic skills and exercises help the retardate in facilitating movement activities throughout the program. Chapter 6, "Working with the Mentally Retarded: Hints and Suggestions," is a guideline for helping the teacher of the retarded to structure a successful activities program. In order to be successful, the program must follow certain criteria that will help the retarded to achieve and fulfill basic needs through motor improvement. Chapter 7, "Suggested Program Activities and Equipment," provides (1) a list of resources for helping the teacher design a movement and rhythmic activities program, (2) procedures for implementing the activities sessions, and (3) lessons and equipment that have been successfully used in the past with mentally retarded persons in a movement and rhythmic program.

Music is a basic factor and, therefore, an important part of the activities session, through songs, records, and/or musical instruments. Goals and objectives of the activities are imperative for each class session but should not render the session inflexible or too structured so that fun and enjoyment in activity participation is destroyed for both the staff and the mentally retarded. Finally, it is extremely important to individualize consistently when considering the needs and capacities of the mentally retarded involved in the activities. Although the participants will all require similar movement and rhythm activities for social, physical, and psychological development, there will be differences in assessment, implementation, and evaluation of each mentally retarded person so that individually they will strive to reach their potentials and become more productive members of society.

Chapter 2

MOVEMENT ORIENTATION

Movement orientation is a means by which the mentally retarded can become acquainted and familiarized with different body movements. Through various movement patterns and skills the mentally retarded may become more physically fit, motorically skilled, and more aware of his individuality through body awareness. Body awareness involves (1) knowing the names of body parts (e.g. elbow, ankle, and shoulder), (2) knowing where these body parts are located in relation to space (kinesthesis), and (3) recognizing sensory sensations that are related to various body parts (e.g. touch and smell).

Before the mentally retarded can be expected to identify, codify, and synthesize the previously listed body awareness components through movement and rhythm, the individual must first become less inhibited, develop skills, and become curious about discovering new movement possibilities. In order to stimulate the retarded individual and prepare him for this discovery approach to movement, a movement orientation program is planned and implemented.

MOVEMENT ORIENTATION ACTIVITIES

Movement orientation activities are needed to help the mentally retarded acquire a movement vocabulary. Before arithmetical equations and concepts can be taught and learned, the individual must first become familiar with the basic relevant terminology in order to understand and use the equations being taught. Also, a basic movement vocabulary is imperative in promoting movement facilitation, communication, and comprehension between the pupil and the teacher. Through certain fun recreational activities, the mentally retarded person can simultaneously begin to acquire the pertinent vocabulary. Categorically, these activities have been divided into three ac-

8

tivity groups: (1) perceptual motor activities, (2) tumbling activities, and (3) physical fitness activities. It is through participation in the three activity groups that the retarded will acquire the terminology to help him know and identify his *self* through body awareness, become stimulated through sensory awareness, and achieve greater physical strength and endurance for overall body conditioning.

Perceptual Motor Activities

The perceptual motor activities in this text are designed to emphasize (1) body awareness, (2) sensory motor development, (3) balance improvement, and (4) muscular integration facilitation.

Body awareness helps the child to identify specific common anatomical parts, e.g. the eyes, ears, and hips. Through activities that call attention to these parts, the retarded learns to associate these various parts within the framework of the total individual. In other words, he learns the concept of "I" and can point out his fingers, his toes, and his knees. Specific activities for promoting body awareness include the following:

*1. Simon Says — a game in which the teacher may choose to play the Simon role and call out various body parts. For example, the teacher may say, "Simon says to point to your toes." The teacher points to his toes, and the children point to their toes. This procedure is continued until eventually the teacher is no longer needed to demonstrate or to help the retarded persons point to their specific body parts. Since the objective of the activity is to learn the various body parts at first, the teacher should not confuse matters by omitting the word Simon before giving a command. That part of the activity can be introduced later when listening skills are being emphasized instead of body part recognition.

*2. Shake and wiggle — to any type of music within a quick tempo; it may be used to stimulate enjoyment and move-

---

*Indicates activities that are recommended for facilitating activity programs that include wheelchair participants and sessions that are integrating handicapped and nonhandicapped persons.

ment. Using the teacher or an aide as a demonstrator, various body parts are wiggled and shaked as the retarded individuals imitate appropriately. Such movements as shaking the hands above the head, to the sides, and toward the ground are successful examples. Other gestures include wiggling the hips, toes, ankles, legs, and heads. If the teacher begins to run out of ideas, the retarded students may enjoy demonstrating a particular shaking movement for the rest of the group to follow. If an individual seems to be uncomfortable or is having problems in leading a shaking movement, then the teacher should be ready to aid or suggest a particular movement to help out the individual and therefore promote achievement.

*3. Name game — an activity that not only involves body awareness, but helps in combining name call recognition with body movement. While seated or standing in a circle, the teacher's name is called out with a simultaneous movement of some body part. If the name is Sally, she might choose to snap her fingers while calling out this name. The activity is repeated two or three times and then the next person proceeds. The rest of the group participates by responding and copying the same movement demonstrated by the person who is being identified by name. Suggestions by the teacher or others in the group may be necessary to aid the shy or troubled individual to remain involved in the activity.

Sensory Motor Activities

These activities emphasize taste, sound, sight, touch, smell, and kinesthesis processes of the human body. Some activities for increasing or heightening the senses would be as follow:

*1. Taste distinction — of the various tastes of the lemon (bitter), pickle (sour), honey (smooth), brown sugar (sweet), and salt.

*2. Smell — distinguishing flower smells, alcohol smells, popcorn smells, and pine tree or other tree smells as appropriate.

*3. Sound — distinctions may be studied by tapping the

floor with different instruments (e.g. spoons, money dropped, lummi sticks), or by tapping different surfaces with the same tool (e.g. the floor, a box, or table top).

*4. Touch — can be discerned by feeling different textures of material swatches, e.g. velvet, cotton, corduroy, silk, and dotted swiss. Also, the retarded can learn to distinguish types of surfaces such as hard wood from a soft surface such as a carpet.

*5. Sight — can be enhanced by distinguishing colors, e.g. red, black, blue, yellow, green, and white. These colors can be located by looking around the room at the walls, chairs, etc. and by noticing different articles of clothing that the retarded persons are wearing during the activities session.

*6. Kinesthesis — the teacher or another participant can blindfold one of the group members. The object is to move the player's arm, leg, or another body part and then return the limb to its original starting point. After the blindfold is removed, the retarded individual must then reenact the identical movement while the manipulator checks to see whether the movement is identical.

Balance Improvement Activities

These activities are categorized into static balance and dynamic balance. Static balance involves movement activities that are motionless or posed (e.g. stork stand). Dynamic balance would involve movement activities that are locomotor, such as hopping across the floor, turning cartwheels, or climbing a tree. Activities that might help to improve the mentally retarded's static balance are the following:

1. Balance board — a device that consists of a circular plywood board approximately 1 inch thick that rests on a fulcrum. The participant must attempt to balance the board completely still without allowing the sides of the board to touch the floor. Once the board is balanced, the

---

*Indicates activities that are recommended for facilitating activity programs that include wheelchair participants and sessions that are integrating handicapped and nonhandicapped persons.

next step is to attempt to maintain static balance for a duration of five to ten seconds with arms crossed and/or eyes closed.

2. Stork stand — an activity that is a basic part of the hop step. The retardate stands on one foot (called the supporting leg) and rests the other foot (called the working leg) on the inside knee of the supporting leg. Both knees should then point in a forward direction. The arms should be extended and held out to the sides for better support in balancing. After the retardate has mastered holding this position for ten seconds, complexity in mastering the skill may be derived by requiring the individual to lift the heel of the supporting leg's foot off the ground and balance for ten seconds. Other variations might include balancing for ten seconds with eyes closed and balancing for ten seconds with the eyes closed and arms folded.

Figure 2-1. Stork stand.

*3. V sit — an activity that requires the retarded individual to balance on his seat while holding the legs, chest, head, and arms off the floor. The arms should be held straight up, over the head, while the legs are extended straight out so that the shape of a V is obtained. This position requires a certain amount of balance and strength, so initially the person may have to be assisted to the V position.

Figure 2-2. V-sit.

4. Other static balance activities would include the following:
   a. Twister — two hands and one foot or two feet and one hand rest on the floor
   b. Head stands — use partners, and begin against a wall
   c. Holding a pose on the balance beam — both high beams and low beams with a partner assisting
   d. Statues — movement to music; when the music stops, all body motion should stop, and the positions should be held like a statue
   e. Hand stands — use partners, and begin against a wall

Dynamic balance activities that might help to improve the retardate's balance are as follows:

1. Hopping steps — this activity requires that the retardate hop on one foot repeatedly in various directions, e.g. forward, backward, sideward, and in turn combinations.

It is required that the student execute the same amount of hops on the left leg as the right leg so that the balance and strength is improved equally for both sides of the body.

Figure 2-3. Hopping steps.

2. Trapeze — an activity in which the individual walks either a chalk line or rope line that is drawn or placed on the floor. If the person becomes comfortable with walking across the straight line, then variations may be made, e.g. requesting a change in directions; varying the steps from a walk to a jump, hop, and/or leap; and winding or zigzagging the rope or chalk line. Variations will present challenge while adding complexity to the activity.

*3. Statues — an activity that involves both static and dynamic balance. Music or a drum may be used to help direct the mentally retarded individual's movement

---

*Indicates activities that are recommended for facilitating activity programs that include wheelchair participants and sessions that are integrating handicapped and nonhandicapped persons.

around the room with some degree of discipline. Instructions may be given that allow the participants to move anywhere they want in the room or that restrict their movement to certain areas of the room. Students may be requested to move fast or slow when the music or drum beat is fast or slow. When the drum beat or music stops, the students must stop immediately and hold whatever pose or position they are in at that time. When the music resumes, the students also begin to move.

4. Other dynamic balance activities might include the following:
   a. Hop-scotch — movement game that requires squares to be drawn on the floor; it includes hops and jumps
   b. Ladder climbing — may initially be practiced by stepping on and off chairs or benches
   c. Stone stepping — use cardboard cutouts or actual stones located on the playground
   d. Balance beam — locomotor movement across a low or high beam

Muscular Integration Activities

Muscular integration activities include eye-hand skills and eye-hand-foot skills. In both the areas of fine and gross motor movements (i.e. small muscle groups and large muscle groups), agility and coordination need to be developed for control and consistency of muscular actions.

Specific motor skills such as eye-hand and eye-hand-foot activities might include the following:

*1. Bean bag throw — may be used with partners, groups, or individuals. Bean bags are easier to catch than balls because they conform to the hands. Objects such as buckets, hula hoops, and/or tires may be used as targets for the projectile being thrown. The students may be given instructions to throw the bag over, through, or into the various targets for diversity.

2. Jumps — are activities that may be executed by the mentally retarded to emphasize coordination skills. Hula hoops, tires, ladders, and/or ropes are types of apparatus

that the participants may jump over, in, between, or on.

Figure 2-4. Jumps.

*3. Balls — are terrific for improving eye-hand-foot coordi-
   nation. Balls may be kicked toward a target with first one
   foot and then the other foot. The participants may
   choose to walk a straight line by shuffling their feet and
   maneuvering a ball across the same line with this shuffling step. Also, the retarded individuals may enjoy sitting in a circle and taking turns kicking the ball or balls
   with their feet to other group members. (Sometimes it is
   fun to use as many as six balls simultaneously with large
   groups.) Bouncing the balls, overhead passing, throwing,
   and pushing a ball using various body parts will help
   improve muscular integration skills.

For the development of total body muscular integration (as
opposed to specific), the following activities are suggested:

1. Jump rope — is an activity that allows each student to work by himself when using a short rope. In addition, a longer rope may be used with two participants holding each end of the rope while two or three other members jump simultaneously or individually.

2. Tinikling — involves the manipulation of two long bamboo poles to a set rhythmic pattern. The participants may begin by jumping over or in and out of the two poles at a height approximately 4 to 6 inches off the ground. Later the height may be increased. The poles are usually manipulated in a three count pattern, the first and second hits (count 1 and 2) are on the floor, and the third hit (count 3) is together. This sequence is repeated continuously. The participants attempt to jump between the poles when the poles hit the floor, and they jump away from the poles before the poles are hit together.

*3. Rope or pole climbing — the equipment is either sus-

Figure 2-5. Rope climb.

pended from the ceiling vertically or suspended horizontally (e.g. parallel bars); this is good for strengthening the upper body parts. The mentally retarded participants should attempt to keep their legs and feet from touching the floor when engaged in climbing or crossing the rope or pole.

4. Other activities for promoting muscular integration include the following:
   *a. Rolling the hula hoops toward a target
   b. Leap frog
   c. Running through, over, and around tires patterned across the floor
   d. Chinese jump rope

Tumbling Activities

Tumbling activities are extremely successful in aiding the participants in a movement orientation program. The mat renders a soft pliable area for movement exploration and experimentation without causing minor bruises and pain that may occur from falls on a harder surface. If standard gymnastic mats are not available, then substitutions can be found by using quilts, blankets, or grassy surfaces. A grass area (yard) is ideal for this type of activity, since it helps get everyone outdoors for some recreational fun.

The following suggested mat activities are fun exercises that enable the mentally retarded to practice and experience a variety of body positions and movements while simultaneously developing strength and muscular coordination.

1. Crawl — involves the stomach and other body parts, as the participant moves in either a forward, backward, or sideward direction.

---

*Indicates activities that are recommended for facilitating activity programs that include wheelchair participants and sessions that are integrating handicapped and nonhandicapped persons.

Figure 2-6. Crawl.

2. Creep — performed on the hands and knees; the upper torso is elevated off the ground.

Figure 2-7. Creep.

*3. Log roll — occurs as the body is stretched out across the mat (fully elongated) and a rolling motion ensues.

Figure 2-8. Log roll.

4. Bunny jump — involves a distribution of weight on the knees and hands; a jumping type movement is used to transport the body across the mat.

Figure 2-9. Bunny jump.

5. Knee jump — the same as the bunny jump except that the weight is distributed only on the knees and not the hands.

Figure 2-10. Knee jump.

*6. Row the boat — performed with the front side of the body down on the mat; weight is distributed on the hands and from the waist down (chest, shoulders, and head are held off the mat by the arms). The body is then dragged across the mat, backward and forward, by using the arms to pull or push the body.

Figure 2-11. Row the boat.

*7. Elbow walk — is a supine position in which the upper back is held up by the elbows that are resting on the mat. The elbows are then moved to transport the body across the mat through a pulling motion.

Figure 2-12. Elbow walk.

8. Kangaroo jump — weight distribution is on the feet and hands. With a jump motion, the body is then transported across the mat.

Figure 2-13. Kangaroo jump.

9. Bear walk — involves the distribution of weight on the feet and hands. Keeping the knees straight, the body then moves across the mat as the right hand coordinates with the right foot, and the left hand coordinates with the left foot.

Figure 2-14. Bear walk.

10. Crab walk — occurs when the back is lifted off the mat by the hand/arms and legs/feet. The body may travel backward, forward, or sideward across the mat.

Figure 2-15. Crab walk.

In addition to individual activities that may be executed on the mat, it is also possible for students to engage in partnering activities. The following activities are examples of partnering activities utilizing the mat:

1. Wheelbarrow — occurs as one partner (A) stands upright and holds the feet of the other partner (B). Partner B is horizontally or diagonally positioned to the mat. B then

uses his arms to direct himself and his partner across the mat.

Figure 2-16. Wheelbarrow walk.

2. Three legged walk — requires a handkerchief. The inside

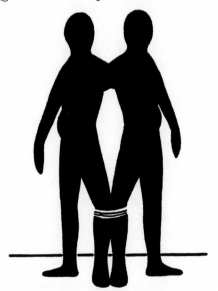

Figure 2-17. Three-legged walk.

legs of the partners are tied, and on command the students attempt to walk or run across the mat together.

3. Bending and rising — requires the two students to sit
   with their knees bent, feet firmly placed on the mat, and
   their elbows locked together. On the count of three, the
   participants attempt to rise and stand up without releasing their arms and elbows from the locked position.
   Lowering their bodies onto the mat is attempted next.
   The trick is to always press the two backs toward each
   other when rising.

Physical Fitness Activities

Physical fitness activities are desirous because they can improve motor skill abilities, muscular control, physique, and
posture. Before the body is capable of meeting the daily and
athletic demands placed on it, a certain fitness level is required,
if only to help prevent injuries and maintain healthy and efficient body functioning.

Muscular strength, flexibility, cardiorespiratory endurance,
and muscular endurance help promote physical fitness. Good
postural habits are the added element that aesthetically improves the overall appearance of the body.

Muscular strength is a muscle or a muscle group's ability to
exert force or work at a given time. Slamming a car door shut, a
jump, or a hop are examples of muscular strength. There are
numerous activities that may be used to increase muscular
strength. Some of these activities are categorized into the following individual activities and partnering activities.

Individual

1. Push-ups build strength in the upper body and arms.
   Females may assume the same position as men; however,
   they should not be forced to lower themselves completely
   to the floor if they do not have sufficient strength. Instead, they should lower their bodies only as far down as
   controllable, before resuming the straight arm position.
2. Heel lifts — slowly lifting and lowering the heels of the

feet. This exercise will help strengthen the leg and feet muscles.

3. Jumps — approximately ten to twelve repetitions will develop strength in the legs and thighs.

*4. Bent knee sit-ups — performed at a moderate to slow pace develop strength in the abdomen muscles.

*5. Pull-ups — require the placement of a high bar above the head of the participants. The hands and fingers grip the bar and then the body is pulled up and away from the ground. This position is then held for as long as possible. (The fingers should be facing the participant's body and not facing away from the body when gripping the bar.)

*6. Swimming — e.g. treading water, floating, breaststroke, and backstroke are only a few exercises for developing total body strength.

7. Running — this may be executed in a forward, backward, or sideward direction to develop strength in the muscles of the thighs, legs, and feet.

*8. Throwing a ball — by using a throw that originates from the chest area and utilizes a two-handed grasp; the muscles of the arms, chest and shoulder girdle are strengthened.

9. Kicking — kicking a ball or kicking the legs frontward and backward repeatedly are two means of developing strength in the leg muscles, stomach muscles, and back muscles.

Partners

*1. Tug-of-war — requires a rope, and partners (or a large group) are placed at either rope end. The objective is for one group to try to pull the other group across a chalk line that has been drawn on the ground to divide the rope in half.

*2. Hand pushing — occurs when partners stand or sit up-

---

*Indicates activities that are recommended for facilitating activity programs that include wheelchair participants and sessions that are integrating handicapped and nonhandicapped persons.

right and place their hands against each other. Taking turns, one participant begins to exert pressure against the other partner's hand that offers resistance by attempting to remain fixed.

3. Inner tube tire pull — requires that two people place themselves in the center of an old, discarded inner tube tire. On command they begin to pull in opposite directions against the tube.

4. Jump rope — needs two assistants to turn the rope while the partners practice jumping rope at the same time with hands held.

Flexibility Exercises

Flexibility exercises help increase the range of motion possible in the joints. Examples of flexibility exercises are the following:

1. Backbends — originating from a supine position on the floor. The participants lift themselves off the floor and hold the backbend position for approximately ten counts.

2. Leg straddles — in a sitting position as the legs are spread out (wide apart) to opposite sides of the body. The head and upper body are then lowered to the right knee and then to the left knee. Knees should eventually be held straight in this exercise; however, at first, the knees will probably be bent.

3. Toe touch — should be performed slowly. The participants keep their knees straight and attempt to touch the floor with their hands and fingers.

Cardiorespiratory Exercises

Cardiorespiratory exercises build overall body endurance that increases oxygen intake into the body and permits the body to remain physically active for a long period of time. Participants without a history of heart problems or other severely debilitating health problems should develop their cardiorespiratory endurance by doing the following:

1. Jogging or running — in short stages of one to two minutes. Eventually, long term goals of fifteen to twenty minutes of continuous jogging should be approached.
2. Jumping rope — for thirty seconds to one minute is the initial plan. Then one should strive to reach a minimum fifteen minutes of continuous rope jumping.
3. Dancing — for fifteen to twenty minutes continuously. Fast or lively musical accompaniment should be used.
4. Swimming — as measured in terms of the number of laps achieved is an excellent exercise. Swimming is especially appropriate for physically disabled mentally retarded persons.
5. Jumping — may be executed against a wall. Participants should strive to touch a point on the wall above their heads while jumping for a minimum of one to two minutes. This exercise may be included as part of the running or dancing program for variety.

Two important factors in developing cardiorespiratory endurance are speed of the movement and length of time involved in the movement. If initially the participants can only continue an activity for thirty seconds before becoming excessively fatigued, then either the activity should be changed at this time or, if necessary, a rest provided; however, weekly increases in activity length should be encouraged to build cardiorespiratory endurance.

Muscular Endurance Exercises

Muscular endurance refers to the number of times a muscle or muscle group can be activated. This deals with repetition of an exercise. The execution of one sit-up or two jumps is not conducive to the development of muscular endurance. Instead, numerous jump repetitions (exceeding a minimum of twelve) is required. Many exercises that help in developing muscular endurance are also used to develop muscular strength, e.g. leaps, sit-ups, and jumps. Additional suggested exercises are as follows:

1. Hopping repeatedly

2. Jumping jacks
*3. Throwing balls at a target
4. Kicking balls aimed at a target
5. Most of the typical calisthenic exercises used in physical education courses

Postural Development Exercises

The development of good postural habits is a necessity for people of all ages and abilities. Although it may not be possible for everyone to exhibit a perfect carriage, straight shoulders, or a flat abdomen, achieving your individual potential is still important and possible. Good posture means that the body is in the process of being more efficiently maintained. The body weight should be evenly distributed over the big toe, little toe, and heel. Knee alignment should be directed between the big toe and little toe as much as possible, since this position affords the most stable support for the knee joint. The spinal vertebrae should be aligned one on top of the other, and the head should continue to follow this vertebral alignment position and not be offset by placement too far forward or backward. Test your posture. In a supine position, see if the lower back is touching the floor when the legs are fully extended and not bent at the knees. The shoulders should also be relaxed and the abdomen muscles working to press the lower back down to the floor. The following suggestions and exercises will aid in achieving and maintaining appropriate postural control.

1. Walking or standing with a book balanced on the top of the head
2. Standing while striving to place the shoulders, back of the head, lower back, and backs of the legs against the wall
3. Exercises to strengthen the lower back and abdomen muscles, e.g. bent knee sit-ups
4. Practice standing with weight equally distributed across the feet, i.e. big toe, little toe, and heel

---

*Indicates activities that are recommended for facilitating activity programs that include wheelchair participants and sessions that are integrating handicapped and nonhandicapped persons.

5. Maintaining the preceding postural alignment while walking across the room.

THE VALUE OF A MOVEMENT ORIENTATION PROGRAM

At this point, the mentally retardate participants and their teacher should begin to feel less awkward and more comfortable with new and old movement experiences. The perceptual motor activities will help heighten the mentally retarded's sense of touch, kinesthesis, taste, smell, and sight. Balance, whether static or dynamic, is a fundamental part of the retardate's existence. Getting into bed, sitting in a chair, and carrying a tray of food are activities that rely on a certain amount of postural balance and control for unaided achievement. Hopefully, through muscular integration activities, tumbling activities, and more general perceptual motor activities, the participants will be exposed to and more aware of the body self. Specifically, they will increase awareness of the eyes, ears, nose, and fingers of the self through participation in recreational opportunities. In order to improve body part identity through more complex and difficult activities, physical fitness is necessary to provide the strength and endurance necessary. As the mentally retarded participants become stronger, they can participate in activities longer and begin to exhibit increased movement efficiency in their everyday body functions. This results with an overall improved condition.

The Council for Exceptional Children and American Association for Health, Physical Education, and Recreation (*Research and Physical Activity for the Mentally Retarded*, 1966) have stated that certain physical objectives for the retarded individual when placed in a recreational setting are an important part of the total development process. Some of these objectives listed are the following:

1. To improve the retardate's general physical health and appearance
2. To develop and improve basic motor skills and such fundamental body movements as walking, running, grasping, pulling, catching, throwing, and kicking
3. To increase physical stamina and motor ability through

the development of specific components of physical fitness that include the following:

a. strength, (muscular) flexibility
b. endurance (muscular)
c. flexibility
d. cardiorespiratory endurance
e. speed
f. agility
g. balance

4. To improve the overall body mechanics of the retardate, i.e. posture, poise, rhythm, and control of movement
5. To improve the function of the sense receptors and the proprioceptors in the retardates' body
6. To develop a more sound body through participation in healthful activities

Chapter 3

MOVEMENT EXPLORATION

MOVEMENT exploration allows the mentally retarded individual to investigate and familiarize himself with new responses and techniques of movement. Movement exploration activities are a means by which the individual can cultivate old and new nonlocomotor and locomotor skills and increase his movement vocabulary while developing more refined body control. Basic movement components have been established through codification. These codified components of movement are comprised of basic steps, gestures, shapes, levels, and direction. In addition, to movement components, qualities of movement, e.g. percussive, sustained, suspension, vibratory, and swinging are the spices that modify, augment, and temper the basic movement components.

Nonlocomotor steps, locomotor steps, basic movement components, and movement qualities are an integral part of any movement activity program. These facets of movement are observed in people's everyday routines, e.g. walking, shopping, and washing, and in sport's events such as football, wrestling, golf, and/or tennis.

Nonlocomotor describes movement that initiates from one point in space (i.e. the floor) and that is fixed or terminates on that same point. Therefore, movement that extends upward into space and returns to the initial starting point is a nonlocomotor activity.

NONLOCOMOTOR ACTIVITIES

Nonlocomotor movement does not necessarily involve highly skilled or complex movement and, therefore, works well with all levels of retardation, including those who are nonambulatory. Examples of nonlocomotor activities are discussed next.

31

*1. Swinging — the movement of a body part in an arc or semicircular pattern with a pendulum effect. That is, when swinging the arm from the shoulder joint, the fingers should draw an arc thru space. Usually the arc is traced repeatedly as the arm moves forward and backward or side to side. Swings may be executed from the shoulder joint, hip joint, fingers, wrists, ankles, and head.

*2. Twisting — the rotation of a body part around its own axis. The head and upper trunk may twist from side to side, the wrist and arm may twist from front and back.

Figure 3-1. Twisting.

*3. Bending — similar to swinging except that it is derived

Figure 3-2a. Bending.

---

*Indicates activities that are recommended for facilitating activity programs that include wheelchair participants and sessions that are integrating handicapped and nonhandicapped persons.

Figure 3-2b. Bending.

from linear angles, whereas swinging is circular and involves curves. Bending the upper trunk towards the floor so that it forms a 90 degree angle with the lower trunk is one example of a linear angle. This nonlocomotor movement is dependent on the type of joints comprising the various body parts being manipulated. The spinal column, wrist, elbow, and knees are possible joint locations capable of producing the bend.

*4. Stamping — action from the foot, leg, and thigh. This occurs when the leg is lifted off the floor and then lowered so that it forcefully strikes the ground. The stamping movement may be produced with either the left foot, right foot, or both feet simultaneously. Stamping is another nonlocomotor movement that can be used with ambulatory or wheelchair retardates who are capable of moving their legs through a lift from the arms.

*5. Clapping — a nonlocomotor movement that involves the hands, forearms, and arms of the body. It may produce noise, depending on the degree of force behind the impact of the two hands coming together. Clapping normally involves simultaneous impact between the right hand and left hand through the use of equal force innervating the muscular action.

6. Balancing — a nonlocomotor movement and is further divided into static balance and dynamic balance. The

stork stand (mentioned in Chapter 2) is an example of static balance. Dynamic balance normally occurs in locomotor movement but may be present in the swinging or bending movement that requires use of dynamic balance in order to (1) produce the movement effectively or (2) keep from falling toward the ground.

7. Falling — relaxation of the antigravity muscles so that the body is lowered to the ground through gravitational pull. The more suddenly the muscles are relaxed, then the more suddenly the fall.

8. Turning — the rotation of the body around its own axis. As long as this movement does not transport the body across the floor, from one point to another, this movement is defined as nonlocomotor.

9. Other types of nonlocomotor movement would include the following:
   a. Stretching various body parts and specifically the limbs
   b. Hanging and swinging from a tree limb or pole
   c. Lifting an object
   d. Throwing a ball
   e. Pushing an object away from the body
   f. Pulling an object towards the body
   g. Kicking a ball or object away from the body

LOCOMOTOR ACTIVITIES

Locomotor activities transport the body from one point on the floor to a different point on the floor. Movement that combines the upward and forward direction is designated as locomotor because the body is transported from one designated point to another. Locomotor movement is often more complex than nonlocomotor movement, partially because it involves more coordination between body parts. Descriptions of commonly used locomotor movements are provided as follows:

1. Walking — or stepping involves the losing and regaining of equilibrium between the antigravity muscles of the body, as the body is transported forward, sideward, or backward. Although walking is not as highly complex

as certain other movement patterns, it does require that the mentally retarded individual work both body part sides equally and utilize a certain amount of dynamic balance so that the walking gait is controlled and efficient in transit. For additional balance control, the participants may practice walking across the floor on tiptoes (heels raised, not touching the floor), which may help improve balance and increase muscular strength in the toes, ankles, and legs.

2. Jumping — a movement from two feet that propels the body upward and off the floor. The landing results when the two feet hit the ground simultaneously. Sometimes the individuals do not understand the mechanics for executing the jump. In this case, it may be helpful to coach the person into bending the knees and, from there, immediately rising on tiptoes. The more the individual pushes into the floor as the knees bend, the more force will be produced for the push-off that propels the body into the air and away from the ground. As a safety precaution for repeated jumps, the knees should always be bent before the jump and during the landing of the jump. This cushioning helps protect the knee joint.

3. Hopping — identical to jumping except that one leg is lifted off the floor so that the takeoff and landing occurs on the same foot. Execution of this movement pattern is the same as in the jump. For clarity and simplicity, locomotor movement that is initiated by one foot with landing on two is described as a jump combination.

4. Leaping — takeoff from one foot (or two feet) with the landing resulting on the opposite foot (or on one foot). Therefore, if takeoff is from the right foot, then landing will occur on the left foot with the right foot held off the ground. This movement may be more complex and difficult than the jump or hop, since it involves the transfer of weight from one foot to the other foot.

5. Running — a series of walks or steps performed at a much quicker or faster pace. The weight of the leg and foot, as it touches the ground (alternating right and left foot) is even so that one foot does not remain in contact

with the ground or in the air for a longer period of time than the other foot.

6. Galloping — a series of running steps, executed in uneven rhythm (*see* Table 1 in Appendix) with one foot maintaining the lead. If the right foot is designated as the lead foot, then the first step commences on the right foot. The left foot then cuts the right foot out of the way and takes the place of the right foot's last position on the floor. In uneven rhythm, the right foot will remain in contact with the floor approximately twice as long as the left foot or vice versa when the left foot takes the lead.

7. Sliding — almost identical to galloping with the exception of the takeoff. The slide promotes a gliding or hovering effect as the feet remain in relatively close contact with the floor. The gallop emphasizes a takeoff upward into space, whereas the slide emphasizes an outward motion. In a slide, it is not unusual for one foot or two feet to remain in contact with the ground at all times, whereas in the gallop one or both feet are often removed from contact with the ground at one stage during the movement.

8. Skipping — when broken down into components is comprised of a step and a hop. Sometimes, when working with the mentally retarded, it may be beneficial to teach the gallop first, then follow with the skip. It is further suggested that the skip be taught from side to side (i.e. alternating from left to right) before commencing with a forward direction.

*9. Turning — may be either locomotor or nonlocomotor. A hop that is turned in place (or revolves around one point) is nonlocomotor; whereas a hop that turns while simultaneously traveling across the floor is considered locomotor. Therefore, it is not the turning or revolving motion that is so important but rather the traveling of the body across the floor.

---

*Indicates activities that are recommended for facilitating activity programs that include wheelchair participants and sessions that are integrating handicapped and nonhandicapped persons.

MOVEMENT COMPONENTS

Movement components are the tools used by the dance choreographer, teacher, and/or coach in the establishment of dances, routines, and/or movement patterns for their players. When the coach requests a player to bend his knees in order to lower the body's center of gravity for more stability, the coach is actually talking about a change in level of the player's body. In this particular case, the player is lowering the level. When the gymnastic coach requires his gymnasts to stretch their limbs and try to occupy or takeup more space with their body, the emphasis is on body shape and/or design relative to the surrounding space. In addition to levels and shape, the dancer may utilize gesture and direction to illustrate moods and emotions or for purposes of communication. Whatever the situation, an analysis of movement will always reveal some, if not all, of the basic movement components mentioned. These basic components are delineated as follows:

1. Space — noted by the shape (e.g. contours) that is made when the body poses or moves through a particular area (i.e. space). Imagine the darkened silhouette of a person's body as it is projected on a white wall or screen. The body is taking up a certain amount of space. There are two ways of analyzing this particular shape: (1) identify the darkened shape according to form and dimension, and (2) look at the white area that surrounds the silhouette. Therefore, it is possible to identify the figure that occupies space and/or the space that surrounds the shape or figure. Finally, when discussing shape, it is also necessary to consider dimension. Is a lot of space taken up, or only a small amount? Is it wide (the figure taking up the space), or is it tall? Is it thin, or is it fat?

2. Level — the placement of the body and body parts using the floor as a reference. If a person stands on a chair, then the body level has been made higher than before. If the body collapses to the floor, then a drastic low level change has occurred. Level changes are necessary in order to help teach the mentally retarded concepts such as low, high, under, and over.

3. Focus — the direction and intensity of the gaze. Not only are the eyes involved, but the direction and level of the head is a part of focus. When the head is lowered, the eyes are usually also focused down; when the head is inclined or turned, then the gaze of the eyes will usually follow accordingly. Change in focus can be a very significant movement, especially when the rest of the body is held motionless. Emphasis in movement of the eyes and head may help the mentally retarded gain more control of the head and eyes and teach customary social exchanges used in various relationships.

4. Direction — commands such as forward, backward, sideward, upward, and downward. It may involve locomotor and/or nonlocomotor movements. Direction is an important movement component because it may facilitate teaching and learning. The individual who does not comprehend directional commands will have difficulty in attempting and completing many locomotor patterns and skills.

5. Gesture — the significant expression of hands, feet, eyes, and larger body part areas for the purpose of communicating a thought, idea, or feeling. Hopefully, gestures should be controlled and then made habitual so that coordination between gestures and verbal communication will occur when appropriate. Vacillation of the articulating wrist of a raised arm for the purpose of greeting is one example of a significant gesture.

MOVEMENT QUALITIES

The final fundamental part of movement exploration is movement qualities. These qualities are the salt and pepper of movement. They augment the impact of movement components in the conveyance of ideas, thoughts, and feelings. The following are movement qualities:

1. Percussive movement — the first example of a movement quality. Movement that is sharp, punctuated, and exaggerated may be described as percussive. Body parts that are significantly involved in demonstrating this quality

are the head, arms, hands, legs, and feet. When two body parts or a body part and a hard object (such as a walking cane) come into contact simultaneously with percussive force, a loud sound, e.g. clapping or stamping may be produced. Percussive movement may be justified in order to get the mentally retarded to move quickly and/or exert extreme amounts of energy or force through a desired body limb or body area.

2. Sustained movement — the antithesis of percussive movement. When percussion is used, the amount of energy innervating the muscle(s) in a given body part is sporadic or intermittent. In other words, the energy is constantly being turned on or off. In sustained movement the energy level must remain constant. Once the energy level is relaxed or turned off, then natural forces such as gravity will produce a change or bring about an entirely new movement. An arm that is perpendicularly positioned to the side of the body at shoulder level is exercising sustenance. This type movement quality may help the mentally retarded develop control and strength for slow movements, since the muscles must resist the pull of gravity in order to maintain this specific arm position.

3. Suspension — the cessation of the energy flow throughout a body part and/or body. It involves a miniscule time period that becomes more significant as strength and control are progressively developed. Suspension may be observed at the pinnacle of a leap or jump. It is that period of time in which the muscles have *ceased* their work of forcing the body away from the ground and *prior* to the time when gravity takes over to bring the body back down to the ground. The higher the individual can jump or leap, and the longer that suspension can exist, then the more significant becomes this particular movement quality.

4. Vibratory movement — clearly observed in the hands and fingers when they are shaken. The amount of energy produced involves a *continuous* intermittent level. Vibratory quality is a voluntary and controlled movement that may also be practiced with the head, feet, legs, and entire

body. Vibratory movement is a different way for the mentally retarded to establish muscular control while expressing themselves during movement exploration.

5. Swinging movement — the last quality. Returning to the idea of the pendulum motion, swinging involves the innervation of muscles to initiate a movement. Momentum then seemingly takes over, until the muscles resume work in order to stop the movement or to repeat the desired movement. Swinging involves movement that is circular; whether a semicircle or a full circle. It also evolves from a specific joint location. Swinging may be smooth, jerky, soft, and/or hard. Swinging may help the participants grasp the concept of circular shapes, as well as establish control and muscular strength.

THE VALUE OF A MOVEMENT EXPLORATION PROGRAM

Movement exploration is an approach for teaching the mentally retarded their body image (both internally and externally), the body's relationship to external objects (e.g. over and under the table), right and left concepts (laterality) while improving coordination and muscular control. Movement exploration should be fun for the mentally retarded. It is up to the teacher to direct the individuals in these new movement experiences through the knowledge and understanding of the basic movement components, which are enhanced by movement qualities.

Chapter 4

DANCE

DANCE is a word that is very difficult to define because of its vast usage and varied meaning. The term dance has been defined by Webster as a movement that is nimble or merry; the act of performing; a social meeting, e.g. a ball. Dance may be used as a verb, "Will you dance with me?" or used as a noun, "Will you go to the dance with me?"

A person may dance around the room, attend a dance, or perform a specific tap dance. The person who performs a dance is called a *dancer*. The actual performance of dance is called *dancing*.

Jean Georges Noverre (1727-1809), a choreographer, dancer, and writer was one of the earliest historians on dance who wrote a series of articles, *Letters on Dancing and Ballet*. Noverre believed that *dancing* was the composition of steps with grace, precision, and time.

Movement has been defined by Laban (1975) as a "feature of all man's activities." Dance and movement are inseparable. "In education, and also in recreation, we build up a dance experience on universal basic forms of movement...," and it is through movement orientation and exploration that a movement repertoire is established that becomes expressed through dance. The similarities between dance and movement are observed in the basic skills, e.g. walk, hop, jump, skip, gallop, and slide. The distinction between dance and movement arises when movement qualities, movement components, and rhythms are combined and experienced. The dancer draws from these three ingredients, organizes, interprets, and expresses life experiences through the language of dance. What differentiates dance from other sports or physical fitness activities? The body itself. In dance, the body is the instrument of movement, not a ball, arrow, rope, or other equipment. The highly technical dancer's body is a well-oiled piece of machinery, refined and capable of producing fantastic shapes, colors, moods, and lan-

41

guage through movement expression.

Dance activities may be psychologically, socially, and physically beneficial in working with the mentally retarded. Through dances that permit self-expression, group interaction, and the development of strength, muscular coordination, and endurance, the mentally retarded person may continue to grow and become an individual who is a productive member of society. There are various types of dance activities in which the mentally retarded can derive benefit and enjoyment simultaneously. These are folk dance, square dance, creative dance, and modern dance. These dance forms do not preclude the advantages and benefits derived from participation in other types of dance forms; however, the specific types mentioned previously have been found to be more fun and conducive to the teaching/learning situation for mentally retarded persons.

Figure 4-1. Dance activities may be psychologically, socially, and physically beneficial, especially in an integrated conga line.

FOLK DANCE

Folk dancing utilizes the basic movement skills from simple

to complex combinations. This type of dancing also provides the participants an opportunity to learn about the customs and beliefs of foreign countries. Dances such as the Mexican La Raspa and the slower Greek Miserlou can be exciting and a recreational means of engaging in the psychological, social, and physical development of mentally retarded persons.

In all folk dances there are basic steps that are executed repeatedly. They may be performed in a circular formation or a line formation. The dances may utilize partners, groups of three or more, or individualized approaches. Whatever combination is chosen, traditionally, the dance will still be comprised of the following basic movements:

1. Schottische — comprised of the step-step-step-hop movement combination. To correctly perform the schottische, the first step is a forward movement; the second step catches up or *closes* next to the lead foot; the third step is another forward movement that then concludes with a hop movement. An example of this dance is right foot step, left foot together (close), right foot step, and right foot hop. Sometimes, learning is facilitated if the schottische is taught in a sideward direction before learning the combination in a forward direction. By performing the schottische once to the right side and then alternating to the left side, the retarded individual is more likely to transfer both his weight and the appropriate foot than when teaching the step combination forward. Later, the schottische may be varied by moving in a backward direction. The most difficult pattern would be to attempt the schottische while turning and with a partner. The schottische is an even rhythm.

2. Polka — comprised of the same steps as the schottische; however, the difference in this movement is found in the rhythm. The polka is performed in an uneven rhythm, whereas the schottische is performed in an even rhythm (*see* Table 2 in Appendix). Therefore, the polka, like the schottische, is a combination of step-close-step-hop.

3. Two-step — a combination of a step-together-step that may begin first on the right foot (Rf) and then with the left foot (Lf). So, if the Rf stepped, the Lf closed next to

the Rf, and the Rf stepped again, a two-step combination would have been executed. The next step would begin with the Lf.

4. Mazurka — a combination of a leap, stamp, and a step movement. The correct sequence is a leap-stamp-step with the right and left foot alternating in the lead position. The rhythm for execution of the mazurka is even and the time signature is generally 3/4. To perform the mazurka, leap onto the Rf, the Lf stamps while closing next to the Rf, and then take a step on the Rf. Continuation of this combination would have the Lf leading next.

5. Waltz — this and the polka are probably the two most difficult combinations for the mentally retarded to learn. The waltz is almost always performed in 3/4 time, and the rhythm is even. The basic components of the waltz are a step-together-step. Again, it is suggested that the waltz be taught to the side while alternating left and right directions. In order to simplify learning, the retardate should practice the waltz individually, then in groups with hands held, and finally with a partner.

Folk dances are a means of studying the traditions, heritage, and social mores of various countries. Records, tapes, and books are readily available to teach folk dances to the mentally retarded; however, it is suggested that the teacher focus on the needs of the retarded individuals when choosing folk dance activities rather than on the specific dances. Modification is an important approach in teaching folk dance steps to the mentally retarded. If the prescribed movements are initially too difficult for the group, then the teacher should change, simplify, or modify these steps so that the participants can enjoy the dances and musical accompaniment while deriving satisfaction and benefit of moving; otherwise, the frustration encountered may preclude movement altogether.

SQUARE DANCE

Square dance is often considered a specific type of American folk dance. Two forms of square dance are the New England

Quadrilles and the Kentucky Running Set (or Appalachian Square) and they are indigenous to specific regions of the United States. Partner dances are predominant in square dance, and a caller is often used to direct the dancers.

The following terms are basic to square dancing. Patterns and partnering descriptions are presented to help the teacher and the mentally retarded to become familiar with simple square dance concepts.

1. Allamande — two persons walk around one another holding identical hands. Usually the caller will signal a left or right allemande.
2. Circle wide — the dancers join hands and form a large circle. Movement direction may be to the left or right.
3. Couple — the two dancers who are working as partners. The female partner normally stands to the right of the male.
4. Corner — the female on the male's left is considered his corner.
5. Courtesy turn — a turn between couples in place. The male takes the female's left hand in his left and places his right hand on her waist as they turn once counterclockwise.
6. Do-si-do — the couple pass each other's right shoulder, circle back-to-back, and return to their original places.
7. Elbow swing — similar to an allemande except that the couple grab elbows (right or left) and swing once around.
8. Grand right and left — the partners face each other and grasp right hands. As each person moves forward to the next person, the left hand is grasped. This movement continues around the circle until the partners meet. In the grand right and left the females move clockwise and males move counterclockwise around the circle.
9. Head couple — the first or lead couple; they are normally positioned with their backs towards the musical apparatus (e.g. record player).
10. Home position — the original or starting position of each couple in the dance.
11. Ladies chain — in a set of four couples, the four ladies

meet in the center and extend their right hands so that they all touch and form a star. The ladies circle clockwise until they are directly in front of the opposite male from home position. The males then execute a courtesy turn and direct the females back to the center, where they form a star, head for home in clockwise direction, and conclude with a courtesy turn.

12. Promenade — position in which the male and female walk around the circle holding hands in front of their bodies in a crossed position. The male normally places his right arm on top.

13. Pass-through — two couples facing each other in the set exchange positions by moving through each other, passing at right shoulders.

14. Set — arrangement of the four couples in a square formation.

15. Shuffle — the walking or stepping movement used in square dancing so that the feet remain in contact with the floor.

16. Side couples — couples two and four in a set of four couples.

17. Star — (right or left hand) occurs as the dancers move into the center of the circle or square and touch hands above heads, forming a star, while continuing to circle in a clockwise or counterclockwise direction.

18. Twirl — used by the male to turn the female. The female's right hand is held overhead by the male's right hand as she takes three or four steps under the arm to complete a full turn.

19. Honors — when the partners acknowledge each other, the females curtsey and the males bow.

Records and books are available that provide simplified instructions on square dances. A few record companies are offering materials that may be used in mainstreaming and in special dance programs for the mentally retarded. Square dancing may utilize line, circle, and the square formations that help in the instruction of shapes and sizes. Depicting each particular formation by placing adhesive tape on the floor will help the mentally retarded visualize the movement direction. Square dancing is loads of fun and has been used successfully with persons in wheelchairs and on crutches.

Figure 4-2. Use of teaching aids, e.g. adhesive tape and partners, when teaching new dance steps.

MODERN DANCE

Modern dance is a highly refined and technical approach to movement, since it emphasizes the muscular development and coordination of body parts for the purpose of exhibiting increased strength and control. This strength and control enables the mentally retarded to respond and execute more difficult and demanding movement positions and combinations. Modern dance is not ballet, tap, jazz, or ballroom dance. Nevertheless, similarity between these dance forms may be observed in certain steps, rhythm, and gestures. Modern dance usually concentrates on the overall development of body parts and is not restricted to exhibition of feet and leg movements as in some other dance forms. Modern dance affords opportunities for self-expression and creativity. Most importantly, modern dance is an art form that can be adapted into a physical education/recreation framework that will help develop the psychological, social, and physical processes of mentally retarded individuals.

Modern dance technique may be categorized into three parts: (1) floor, (2) standing-nonlocomotor, and (3) locomotor movements. Both the floor and standing exercises primarily warm the body, render the body supple and flexible, and develop strength. This is achieved through exercises that strive to strengthen and stretch the isolated muscle groups and body parts. The floor exercises focus on the stretching, contracting, and releasing the muscle action while utilizing the immovable floor surface for resistance. The standing nonlocomotor exercises also emphasize stretching, contracting, and releasing of muscle action plus integration of balance coordination.

The locomotor combinations stress the integration of specific motor or movement patterns. The locomotor exercises propel the body through space, help establish a collaboration between rhythm and movement, and essentially allow the body to articulate and communicate.

Body communication through dance is the means by which an individual's moods, feelings, and creative expression are overtly manifested. In the modern dance course, dancers may design compositions of solo or group pieces that offer the opportunity for self-expression while simultaneously teaching the students to evaluate and appreciate modern dance as an art form.

Modern Dance Nomenclature

The following proposed syllabus and dance terminology offers basic components that are a part of the modern dance class.

1. Locomotor movements — transport the body from one place to another. Basic locomotor movements to be used in the dance program with the mentally retarded may consist of the following:
   a. Hop — elevation upward from one foot and landing on the same foot
   b. Jump — elevation upward from two feet and landing on two feet
   c. Leap — transfer of weight from one foot to the opposite foot with elevation in between

    d. Gallop — step coupé (cutting step where one foot replaces the other) or two steps in uneven rhythm with one foot remaining in the lead (elevation upward)

    e. Slide — similar to a gallop sideward, but there is a gliding motion rather than elevation, and at least one foot is always in contact with the ground

    f. Skip — a repeated step-hop

    g. Polka — a step-close-step-hop (uneven rhythm)

    h. Schottische — step-close-step-hop (even rhythm)

    i. Mazurka — leap-stamp-step (even rhythm)

2. Nonlocomotor movements — stationary, i.e. the body is not transported. The basic nonlocomotor movements are the following:

    a. Swinging

    b. Bending

    c. Twisting

    d. Stretching

    e. Collapsing

    f. Falling

    g. Turning

Dance technique develops as certain motor skills (exercises) pertinent to the dance, are learned and practiced. Basic modern dance technique includes the following:

1. Plié — bending of the knees. The dancer lowers the body

Figure 4-3. Plié.

slowly with the knees aligned over the five toes and then resumes standing position. The movement throughout the execution of the plié is continuous, and at no time does the body rest in the deep knee bend position.

2. Relevé — to rise on the balls of the feet. Again, as in plié, the knees should be aligned over the five toes as the heels are lifted off the floor.

Figure 4-4. Relevé.

3. Tendu — the toe pointed and the instep (top of the foot)

Figure 4-5. Tendu.

stretched. The toes should not be curled.

4. Dégagé — similar to the tendu except that the toes do not maintain contact with the floor. As the foot brushes, the toes are extended two to four inches off the floor. This exercise strengthens toes and improves flexibility in the ankle joint.

Figure 4-6. Dégagé.

5. Turns — a pivot on one foot or two in which a 360 degree rotation occurs. When a step, run, etc., is added between turns, the movement pattern may become locomotor.

6. Fall — initially taught from a kneeling position. The antigravity muscles are relaxed as gravity lowers the body to the floor. The arms are used to catch the falling body and lower it to the floor.

7. Arabesque — a pose on one leg. The supporting leg (leg holding the body up) is perpendicular to the floor. The knee of the working leg is kept straight.

Figure 4-7. Arabesque.

8. Attitude — the same as an arabesque except the working leg knee is flexed or bent.

Figure 4-8. Attitude.

9. Lunge — one knee is bent while the other is straight. The upper body (head, shoulders, back, and pelvis) is then positioned over the bent knee.

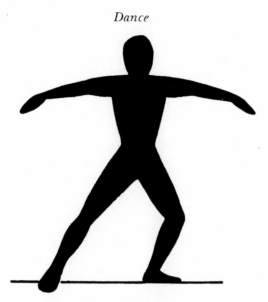

Figure 4-9. Lunge.

10. Dance walk — an even rhythm pattern in which there is alternate transfer of weight as one foot takes a step and then the other. In this type of walk the toes touch the ground first, then weight is distributed across the ball of the foot and to the heel.

11. Assemblé — a special type of jump in which the spring occurs from one foot and the landing results when two feet hit the floor simultaneously.

12. Sissone — another type of jump in which the spring occurs from two feet and the landing is on one foot.

13. Triplet — a movement in 3/4 time that consists of a plié and two relevés. The steps are plié Rf, relevé Lf, relevé Rf, and the lead foot alternates.

14. Polka — usually performed in 2/4 time in an uneven rhythm. The components of the step are a step Rf, close Lf, step Rf, hop on the Rf, or hop-step-close-step.

15. Schottische — the same as the polka step except that the rhythm is even.

16. Pas de basque — performed in an even 3/4 count and

consists of a leap-step-step.

17. Mazurka — performed in an even 3/4 count and consists of a leap-stamp-step.

CREATIVE DANCE

Creative dance, whether treated as an entity or as an integral part of modern dance, is movement that provides the mentally retarded person an opportunity to express himself motorically. This expression may result in a form of individualism — introspection with oneself exhibited through movement. It may also take place through group interaction, i.e. expression based on relationships, attitudes, and feelings between the group participants as it is revealed through the dance movement.

In order for the dance to be designated as creative it prohibits direction from the typical choreographer/dancer structure or format pertinent to other dance forms. Instead, there is a facilitator or motivator in place of a choreographer whose function is to warm up (or prepare), activate, and help evaluate the end result — the dance. The particular parts of a creative dance — preparation, activation, and evaluation — with regards to the mentally retarded are discussed as follows:

1. Warm-up — a necessary prelude to beginning a creative dance experience. This section presents the theme, i.e. the idea being expressed. The theme may be based on food items, mechanical toys, trees, flowers, or the family washing machine. Other themes may deal with a particular song, nursery rhyme, poem, or narration. Any of these concepts are possible themes for a creative dance; however, it is important in the warm-up that the teacher help the individual to bring out important features and characteristics that are inherent in the theme. Some simple questions from the teacher based on texture, sounds, function, shape, changes, size, locomotor and nonlocomotor movement, type of movement, and rhythmic features should be brought to the dancer's attention in concise and exemplified terms. An example is the creative dance "popcorn." First, it is necessary to discuss, feel, and see the subject material (popcorn ker-

nels). The teacher should propose such thought questions as the following: are the kernels hard or soft? Round or square? Small or large? When they are poured into the popcorn popper do they jump into the pan or do they land softly? Are the kernels close together or far apart? When the oil is added, are the kernels greasy or sticky? Do they slide around the popper, or do they stick close together? As heat is applied, what happens to the oil? Do the kernels remain quiet, or do they begin to move around the pan? What happens when the kernels begin to explode? Do they bounce or slide around the popper? Do they remain hard, or do they become soft? Do the kernels expand, or do they utilize the same amount of space as before they began to pop around the pan? Finally, do the kernels become compact and snug or scattered and loose in the popper?

These questions are only suggestions that help call the dancer's attention to the subject being discussed and to the qualities and characteristics they will explore through the dance movement. It teaches them how to use space and how to interpret the movement. The dance should allow the dancer to self-express and to occupy space without encroachment on the involved group members' space.

2. Activation — the implementation of the concept or subject into movement. It is the enactment of everything that has been discussed in the warm-up activity. The teacher by now should have prepared and motivated the dancers for the appropriate movement that will be required in the dance. Although there is no absolute right or wrong steps in performing the dance, some movement could be designated as more appropriate than other movements. A dancer who jumps and hops around the room after the popcorn was completely popped should be made to realize the nonlocomotor movement would probably be more appropriate at this stage. A suggestion for the teacher is to discuss (not tell) the possible sequential steps in the various scenes with the dancers, before letting the group perform the dance. This discussion should

attempt to cover succinctly appropriate and inappropriate movement when it applies. Furthermore, it is usually a good idea to establish the concept of a dance *beginning* and a dance *ending* before performing the dance. It is not necessary that all the participants start and end simultaneously or identically, but it is necessary that they establish for themselves a starting place in the room at which to begin the dance and a concluding pose to ensure finalization. This procedure will help maintain a framework for the dancers and will impede movement that is random and superfluous.

3. Evaluation — may be used (1) as a means of calming the dancers at the conclusion of the activity session, (2) as a means for allowing discussion and interpretation by the dancers on the activity that took place (did they follow the theme sequentially and comprehensively), and (3) as a means by which the teacher can analyze whether her objectives were met through the dancer's performance of the dance.

At the conclusion of the dance activity, the mentally retarded participants may be excited and overly enthusiastic. By sitting the dance members on the floor, the teacher can talk with them and allow a quiet time to absorb the feeling and moods expressed throughout the activity period.

If the teacher wishes to explore the comprehension and/or realization of the basic concept(s) revealed through the dance on the part of the retardates, then a question/answer period or discussion period may be appropriate. Discussion also may help some of the dancers attempt to express their individualized dance movement through verbalization, which provides another means for communicating feelings and moods other than through the nonverbal modality.

Through the discussion period, the teacher can further analyze the individuals for insight and their fulfillment of the predetermined objectives. Whether the teacher attempts to evaluate the aggregate group movement in the dance or attempts to analyze each individual member within the group is probably not as important as evaluating whether or not the group and/or individuals fulfilled the predetermined student objectives. These objectives may be based on (1) the individual's socialization needs (such as learning to occupy space without bumping needlessly into the other members), (2) the ability to express oneself or to lose inhibitions, (3) the ability to follow predetermined movement concepts sequentially, (4) the ability to listen to and follow directions within the boundaries established by the structural framework and (5) the overt expression of self through a mode that is enjoyable and recreative.

Whatever concept is selected, whatever accompaniment is chosen, and whatever dance activity is performed, the emphasis must still be placed on the end result — the fulfillment of objectives — and not on the perfection of dance steps, precision, and rehearsed reiteration of choreographed steps by one individual.

Written objectives for the dance program will probably be concerned with one or all of the four *movement analysis* parts listed as follows:

1. What we move — with regards to the body or an object
2. How we move — with regards to movement quality (percussive, vibratory, sustained, suspended, swinging)
3. Where we move — with regards to space, direction, and level
4. With whom we move — with regards to the interrelationship of group members (Robinson, Harrison and Gridley, 1970)

The following are suggested themes and topics that may be helpful in choreographing dances.

1. Word usage
   a. Individual dancer's name
   b. Rhymes (nursery)
   c. Expressions (oh, u, ow, ugh)
2. Body part usage
   a. Indicate through movement five body parts that say hello
   b. Perform a creative dance that depicts a lawn mower cutting the grass
3. Animals, insects, dolls, toys
4. Props

   a. Scarves
   b. Balls
   c. Streamers
   d. Shawls
   e. Hats
5. Food
   a. Popcorn
   b. Taffy
   c. Jello®
   d. Creamy fudge
   e. Ice cream
6. Games
   a. Simon says
   b. Card game
   c. Twister

THE VALUE OF DANCE

Although the term *dance* may be a complex and difficult term to define, its existence may create self-expression, creativity, enrichment, physical development, and social opportunities for many mentally retarded persons. Each group member is considered an individual and a dancer. Each dancer is considered a group member. Dancing can help people mix socially, make friends, and reduce shyness in a recreational environment that promotes desirable conduct. In addition to being an important leisure-time activity, dance also encourages the development of positive social skills such as courtesy and appropriate manners.

Dance perpetuates the cognitive and physical development of the mentally retarded that is taking place in the education classroom. Folk dance teaches history; creative dance teaches art; square dance may highlight mathematics; and modern dance helps coordination, rhythm, and overall physical development.

Finally, dance provides opportunities for achievement that may promote self-worth, a knowledgeable body-image, and a positive self-concept. It is a recreational opportunity that enhances life's experiences through the learning of new skills and

primarily directed towards isolated body parts are the following:

where   represents movement steps (duration)

1. "If You're Happy and You know It, Clap Your Hands"
2. "One Finger One Thumb"
3. "Clapping Land"
4. "In a Cottage In the Woods"
5. "The Bus"
6. Washing songs

Action songs may also involve total body coordination that ranges from simple to complex movement. Examples of these songs are as follow:

1. "Old Brass Wagon"
2. "Looby-loo"
3. "Pop Goes the Weasel"
4. "Bluebird"
5. "Mexican Hat Dance"
6. "Yankee Doodle"
7. "Skip to My Lou"
8. "London Bridge"

Action songs involving gross body coordination are often described as simplified circle dances or partnering dances, since they are usually performed by couples or in a large circle. However, it is usually best to (1) teach the words and melody to the retarded individual first, (2) teach the dance steps and/or actions together without partners or in groups, and (3) combine and practice the song and dance steps through group participation or partners.

RHYTHM INSTRUMENTS

Rhythm instruments can be expensively purchased from a music shop, hand made from materials found in the home or classroom, or modified from old pots, pans, wastepaper baskets, and/or plastic food containers. As long as the apparatus is capable of producing a sound, then it will suffice for a rhythmic instrument. Basic instruments found in a rhythm band are as follow:

1. Tambourines — that can be made from pop bottle caps threaded onto a stiff coat hanger that rattles when shaken.
2. Drums — that can be found around the home or classroom by turning a wastepaper basket upside down and beating on the bottom with either the fingers or a durable stick. Pencils will function sufficiently as drumsticks, or small dowels approximately 12 inches in length may be purchased.
3. Shakers — maracas may be purchased at music stores. Shakers may be made by placing kernels of dried corn or dried beans in a plastic food container and/or plastic bottle (e.g. a bleach bottle). Variations in sound may be produced by changing the size of the container, by changing the type of container (i.e. metal as opposed to plastic), and by changing the different contents (e.g. dried peas, pop bottle caps, paper clips) as well as altering the amount of the contents within the container.
4. Sticks — pencils, wooden dowels (approximately 12 inches in length), and sawed off broom handles are another source of rhythm instruments. The sticks should come in pairs and may be struck against one another, rubbed together, or used as drumsticks.
5. Sandblocks — easily made by covering two erasers or two wooden blocks (4 inches by 4 inches by 4 inches) with sandpaper. When the two covered blocks are rubbed together, the sandpaper produces a scraping sound.
6. Bells — can be obtained by purchasing several loose bells from a store and then stringing these bells together on a piece of ribbon and elastic for easier handling.
7. Other instruments — whistles, clappers, and triangles are

also available for purchase. These instruments, when combined with the other instruments listed previously, become parts of the rhythm band. By adding recorded music, e.g. marches, polkas, and waltzes, the group members can practice using their instruments to accompany the tempo of the songs as well as learning to distinguish between even and uneven rhythms. Challenges become more complex when the retardates attempt to play their instruments and accompany a specific song while moving around the room performing the march, skip, polka, or waltz.

Figure 5-1. Guitar music alone or in combination with art activities promotes good listening skills.

PARACHUTE AND OTHER ACTIVITIES

Parachute activities are a tremendous success within a program, especially when used as a beginning or culminating activity. The mentally retarded enjoy manipulating the chute by lifting, shaking, pulling, and stretching the apparatus to musical accompaniments with varied rhythms. This type of activity primarily involves group participation and therefore can be used to perpetuate social development in addition to rhythm abilities.

The following activities are suggested as approaches to facilitate group cooperation, friendship, and rhythm games.

1. Recognition of names — each participant stands and holds onto the parachute. In order to facilitate the recognition of names, name tags with either first or first and last names written should be provided and placed on each member. On the count of three, everyone lifts the parachute high into the air above the head. At first, everyone can disengage one hand from the parachute in order to wave to other group members who are visible beneath the suspended parachute. Second, as the parachute is lifted again, one person should be singled out from the rest. This person is acknowledged by name as everyone in the group waves and signals a "hello (*name*)" to the individual. This exercise should be repeated until everyone within the group has been singled out and acknowledged by name. It is important that everyone be recognized; therefore, if time is limited, it is advised to call out two or three individuals as a group instead of omitting some of the members entirely.

   This particular type parachute activity is beneficial in (1) promoting self-awareness, (2) providing positive attention with one or more persons, (3) establishing recognition of self-worth and importance, and (4) providing an opportunity for the mentally retarded persons to recognize others and develop relationships.

2. Circle dances — exciting and enthusiastic rhythm activities that are also helpful in promoting socialization. La Raspa is a Mexican dance that may be modified for use with both wheelchair and nonwheelchair persons. The musical phrasing helps in dictating the number of times a step is repeated in the dance. Basically, the dance consists of three hopping steps, three counts of shaking the parachute, and sixteen sliding steps or gallops to the right, and then the dance is repeated to the left. This sequence is followed until the music concludes. The dance steps are explained in detail as follows:

a. The steps begin with the right foot (Rf), changing to the left foot (Lf), and then back to the Rf with a one count rest added at the end. The progression is Rf-Lf-Rf-rest. As the Rf extends forward, the heel is placed on the floor approximately 12 inches in front of the Lf. The Lf heel is extended, then the Rf heel is extended with a pause.

b. As the Rf holds its last position, the fingers and arms then begin to shake the parachute on the counts 1-2-3 and rest on count 4. The progression is shake-shake-shake-rest.

c. The steps a and b are then repeated except that the Lf begins instead of the Rf. The dance steps for a and b are repeated four times before the next part of the dance occurs.

d. The entire group, holding onto the parachute, marches, skips, gallops, slides, etc., halfway around the circle, starting to the right. After sixteen counts this step is then repeated to the left for sixteen counts.

e. At this point the entire dance starts over.

    For wheelchair persons, the same music is used; however, depending on the capabilities of the group, more shaking, twisting, and lifting of the parachute (concentrating on movement from the waist up) may substitute for the locomotor steps, e.g. sliding, galloping, and hopping.

3. Singing circle dances — appropriate fun activities that provide an opportunity for the dancers to integrate verbal responses with gross motor responses. "The Old Brass Wagon" is a song that has corresponding dance steps. The parachute is important in this particular instance because it helps facilitate recall and keeps everyone together and moving in the correct direction, i.e. as long as everyone maintains hold of the parachute. It is especially helpful to place key persons at various locations around the parachute who know the dance to serve as prompters. As the teacher and key persons move to the right or left, the rest of the participants will easily follow this same line of direction, decreasing confusion for everyone in the early stages of learning the dance.

Figure 5-2. Parachute activities are versatile teaching aids that can be used with large groups.

Rhythmic activities can be fun and simultaneously educational for the participating retarded individuals. Through the use of lively and enthusiastic rhythms, some of the most lethargic and passive individuals will become excited and less inhibited in their responses. Quiet and calm rhythm activities, especially when added to a soft and flowing musical accompaniment, can help in providing a relaxed environment for those individuals who are normally overactive throughout the day. Through the rhythmic activities the mentally retarded can practice counting, whether through striking a drum sixteen times successively or through learning to kick three times in a dance step and rest on the fourth count. Vocabulary can be increased in songs that range in subject matter from animals to the more modern *Star Wars* themes and such concepts as directionality and laterality.

Other rhythmic activities that have been used successfully with the mentally retarded are discussed as follow:

*1. Lummi sticks — come in pairs and are usually manipulated by the fingers and hands. The finger/hand position is usually 2 to 4 inches from the end. The sticks may be used to tap out rhythms on the floor, drums, or on various body parts. Tapping the shoulders lightly with the sticks is an excellent way of continuing a steady rhythm while giving instructions simultaneously. It is possible that only one lummi stick should be used initially if the participants are having difficulty synchronizing two at once.

The sticks may be used in front of the body, to the sides of the body, behind the body, and over the head of the body. Lummi sticks provide help in the development of directionality, laterality, and coordination abilities with rhythms.

The following terminology was developed by Bryant and Oliver (1967) for instructing lummi stick activities.

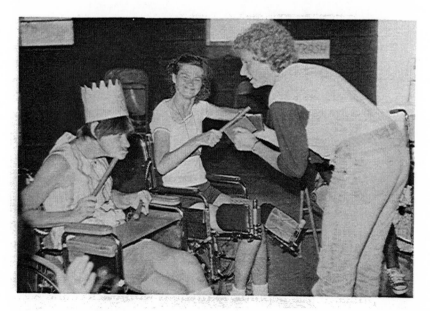

Figure 5-3. Lummi sticks help develop fine motor coordination in rhythm activities.

---

*Indicates activities that are recommended for facilitating activity programs that include wheelchair participants and sessions that are integrating handicapped and nonhandicapped persons.

a. Down — both sticks are held vertically and tap the floor.
b. Together — sticks are held horizontally and tapped simultaneously.
c. Right — both sticks tap to the right side of the body.
d. Left — both sticks tap to the left side.
e. Side — a stick in the right hand taps the right side while a stick in the left hand taps the left side concurrently.
f. Shoulders — lightly tap the shoulders with the sticks.
g. Brush — hold sticks vertically and rub them together back and forth.
h. Flip — tap the floor with the sticks, flip, and catch the opposite end.
i. Pass — lay the stick on the floor next to a neighbor and pass one stick on.

"Alley Cat," "The Beat Goes On," "Yellow Submarine," or almost any 4/4 music with a consistent tempo is ideal accompaniment. One example of a combination using four of the previously listed terms would be the following:

Together - 2 - 3 - 4 - 5 - 6 - 7 - 8
Right - 2 - 3 - 4 - 5 - 6 - 7 - 8
Left - 2 - 3 - 4 - 5 - 6 - 7 - 8
Shoulders - 2 - 3 - 4 - 5 - 6 - 7 - 8

Shortening the number of repetitions, increasing the number of different terms, and adding more complex movements will challenge even the best rhythm performers. If frustration is a problem, however, only one stick should be used, repeat each movement at least sixteen times before changing, and use persons strong in rhythm as models.

2. Tinikling poles — long bamboo poles that are used primarily for stepping to rhythms with the feet and legs. The two poles are held at each end by a volunteer who is then responsible for maintaining the rhythm. Time signatures of 3/4 or 4/4 are usually appropriate, and musical accompaniment must maintain consistency and

steadiness.

Individuals or groups of two, three, or four may jump in and out of the sticks together. Rhythmic patterns may include the two poles hitting the floor once, and together twice, for example, (1) down, (2) together, (3) together. The dancers would jump in between the poles on the count one and out on counts two and three.

3. Chinese jump ropes — thin elasticized bands (like large rubber bands) that may be placed around the ankles, knees, or waists and stretched between two volunteers. As the band is stretched between the two volunteers, one end can be turned over, making a crisscross pattern (or X). Individuals or couples may attempt to jump over the rope as the distance from the floor to the band is increased.

The Chinese jump ropes may also be manipulated by the volunteers who will now serve as dancers. A hop and jump are the basic steps used as the two dancers stretch the bands taut around their ankles or knees (in an uncrossed position). On the count of one both dancers hop on the Lf while pointing the Rf in front of the body and under the edge of the band. On the count of two the Lf hops again while the Rf crosses the edges of the band. This step is then repeated several times before alternating with the Rf hopping.

4. Ball rhythms — good for illustrating the concept of round, as compared with rectangles or squares. Ball rhythms utilize large muscle groups in arms and legs. Rhythm activities can be conducted with the participants seated on the floor or in chairs or standing. Balls may be kicked with the feet, pushed with or bounced off the head, and thrown, pushed, or caught with the hands. In the beginning the balls should be large and soft. Foam balls are great for mentally retarded persons who have major coordination problems. Records are available that uses music to accompany ball rhythm activities. These activities may be used for individualized instruction, in partners, and/or in large groups. One idea is to have twelve to fourteen participants seated in a circle. Get at

least six balls going around the circle while the participants kick the balls that come toward them. The kick should be fast or slow, depending on the tempo of the music.

5. Rhythmic physical fitness routines — performed to music are great for motivating the participants to move while developing rhythmic awareness and learning rhythmic skills. A few calisthenics that have been used in rhythmic physical fitness routines include the following:
   a. Jumping jacks
   b. Bent knee sit-ups
   c. Slow toe touches (or knees in most cases)
   d. Horizontal arm rotations
   e. Running in place
   f. Leg kicks to the front and to the back
   g. Head rolls

6. Jump rope rhythms — good for the mentally retarded because they are allowed to learn and practice an activity that is used often in the everyday play of many non-handicapped children. Music and/or chants should be taught and used so that rhythm will be emphasized in the tempo or cadence. An example of a chant that could be taught is the following:

   Cinderella dressed in yellow
   Went upstairs to see her fellow
   How many kisses did she get;
   1 - 2 - 3 - 4 - 5 - 6 - 7 - 8

   Jump rope routines promote individual or group play, develop body strength and endurance, and facilitate learning in the area of rhythms.

7. Clapping or hand rhythms — the final activity and no equipment is necessary for this rhythms activity. Clapping, snapping, and slapping utilize the fingers and hands in establishing certain rhythm patterns. Challenges occur when the three elements are combined and complicated rhythmic patterns ensue. Verbal games, using the clapping, snapping, and/or slapping actions are fun for group play, especially with a verbalized chant. Suggested activities include the following:

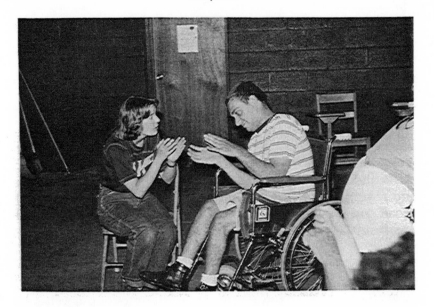

Figure 5-4. Clapping activities are beneficial for both ambulatory and nonambulatory persons.

```
snap - 2 - 3 - 4 - 5 - 6 - 7 - 8
clap - 2 - 3 - 4 - 5 - 6 - 7 - 8
slap - 2 - 3 - 4 - 5 - 6 - 7 - 8
snap - 2 - 3 - 4
clap - 2 - 3 - 4
slap - 2 - 3 - 4
snap - 2
clap - 2
slap - 2
snap -
clap -
slap -
snap -
clap -
slap -
```

Try enunciating the word with the corresponding action.

VALUE OF RHYTHM

Rhythm is a means whereby the mentally retarded can learn to move and participate with group members in unison. It may reduce randomness and help develop self-direction. Rhythmic activities stimulate the mentally retarded's auditory, tactile, and kinesthetic senses through play and group interaction.

Parachute activities, action songs, rhythm instruments, lummi sticks, jump rope, and certain body movements present many varied opportunities for the development of rhythmic skills and abilities. People's interests and hobbies vary greatly, and rhythmic activities provide a multisensory tool that is very broad and flexible. The individual who dislikes dance may find great satisfaction in ball rhythms and/or physical fitness routines.

Rhythms are a fundamental part of any movement program. Rhythm is a way of life; it is observed in our breathing, walking, speaking, and gesturing. Helping one to develop directed and controlled rhythms is an important part of successful play and leisure participation.

Chapter 6

WORKING WITH THE MENTALLY RETARDED: HINTS AND SUGGESTIONS

THE teacher of the mentally retarded is probably the most vital part of their total educational process. Successful programming for the mentally retarded relies on the teacher's leadership abilities as initiator, interpreter, and evaluator. The selected activities, equipment, and facilities serve as tools in the total process. The competent teacher must be prepared in order to help the mentally retarded strive for achievement. Preparedness is possible when the teacher (1) is aware of, sensitive to, and able to address the needs of the mentally retarded individuals who are involved in the program; (2) has established tangible goals and objectives for the activity ses-

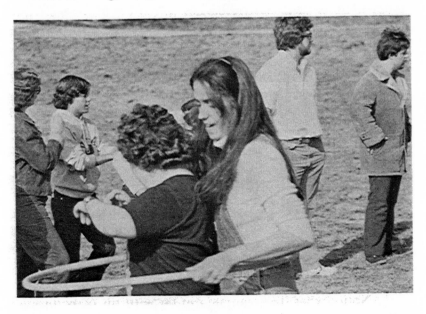

Figure 6-1. The teacher must be aware of, sensitive to, and able to address needs of the mentally retarded participants.

73

sions; and (3) has researched and utilized possible resources in which to obtain ideas and pertinent information, necessary to increase knowledge and to broaden the scope of activities, that will best fit the needs of the mentally retarded.

Bertha E. Schlotter and Margaret Svendson (1951) have listed similarities between retarded and nonretarded individuals, as well as the following suggestions for structuring a program that are still being used in the 1970s.

1. Mental age seems to be a more important factor than chronological age in determining interests and abilities of the mentally retarded.
2. Color coded symbols, e.g. Xs or word/direction signs posted around the room, around the floor, and on the participants are helpful teaching tools.
3. The course of development of interests, especially play, in the mentally retarded is similar to nonretarded except that the rate of development is usually slower.

When establishing a program for the mentally retarded that is based upon their psychological, physical, social, and emotional development through an environment that is recreational and positive in nature, the teacher must consider (1) teacher objectives for a successful program, (2) pupil objectives for a successful program, (3) activity selection, (4) adaptation of activities to fit the needs of each individual, and (5) criteria for program evaluation. These necessary components of successful programming for the mentally retarded, are described and discussed in this chapter.

TEACHER OBJECTIVES

When preparing for a particular activity session or program, it is important for the teacher to have established goals and objectives. Initially these goals and objectives are teacher directed to provide a framework in which the teacher will work. The following are therefore the teacher's responsibility.

1. Notice what the retardate can do with his body through assessment. The "Movement Checklist" (*see* Table 3 in Appendix) is an example of an assessment that may be used to determine strengths and weaknesses.

2. Observe what the retardate is able to understand of movement by determining the extent of the movement repertoire. (*see* Table 4 in Appendix)
3. Strive to plan *with* the individual and adjust for disabilities; try not to plan *for* the individual.
4. Be prepared for trial and error situations.
5. Keep verbal directions at a minimum without talking down to the participants. Use facial expressions to accentuate or punctuate verbiage.
6. Be patient.
7. Try to establish an environment that is free from rigidness or tenseness.
8. Be aware of necessary safety factors before the activity begins.
9. Offer positive leadership.
10. Be prepared for weather changes and check equipment for proper functioning.
11. Plan ahead in order to be prepared for resolving or avoiding unnecessary problems.
12. When possible, avoid failure and frustration. Instead promote success.
13. Provide genuine praise and encouragement without satiation.
14. Remember, you are a model, and many mentally retarded persons are natural imitators. (*Recreation and Physical Activity for the Mentally Retarded*, 1966.)

PUPIL OBJECTIVES

After teacher objectives have been considered, the second step is to establish goals and objectives for the mentally retarded who will be involved in the various activities. In other words, what will be expected of the participant involved in the activities? What will be his role and predicted results from participation? Such goals and objectives might be based upon the following:

1. To improve the general physical health and appearance (both health and posture) of the individual.
2. To improve poise and control of movement and/or overall body mechanics.

3. To have social experiences that will aid in the pursuit of increasing degrees of social independence.

Figure 6-2. Movement and rhythm activities in an integrated recreation setting promote social experiences.

4. To develop better self-care skills.
5. To become a better citizen and contributing member of society.
6. To increase friendships and acquaintances; to be friendly and outgoing.
7. To improve one's general self-image and increase or develop self-respect.
8. To release aggression in socially acceptable ways.
9. To learn to accept evaluation, direction, authority, and constructive criticism.
10. To achieve means of self-expression through nonverbal ways.
11. To improve their communicative vocabulary (whether through words or movement).
12. To increase attention span and the ability to concentrate.
13. To improve their ability to listen and follow directions.

14. To develop vocational skills.
15. To arouse the sense of curiosity and inquisitiveness.
16. To acquire hobbies, skills, interests, and lifetime values.
17. To develop latent or untapped talents.
18. To improve sensory discriminative powers.
19. To increase the comprehension of skills and abstraction abilities.
   (Recreation and Physical Activities for the Mentally Retarded, 1966)

ACTIVITY OBJECTIVES

A third consideration within the program structure is the activities prescribed for each lesson. The following considerations should be made in order to make the appropriate selection of activities.

1. Know what the activity is for, i.e. purpose. Examples are the following:
   a. Motivation and stimulation of the mentally retardates' curiosity and inquisitiveness
   b. Improvement of desirous skills and abilities
   c. Leisure or play opportunities for recreational purposes
   d. Social behavior — group interaction activities to improve manners, e.g. courtesy, responsibility
   e. Improvement of health through physical fitness activities
2. The activity should be practical
   a. appropriate facilities (space, proper equipment, safe equipment) is available for the type of activities chosen
   b. a sufficient amount of time should be anticipated and allocated
   c. consider the people involved, i.e. the participants, staff, volunteers
3. The activity should be challenging.
4. Competition should be promoted within the framework of cooperativeness among all those involved.
5. The activity should be socially beneficial.
6. Action and total group participation is the ultimate goal.

7. The activity should be adaptable to everyone — physically handicapped, emotionally disturbed, and/or mentally handicapped.

ACTIVITY SELECTION

When the teacher has considered and accounted for the necessary goals and objectives of the program, the next step is to select the activities to be used. The following are suggestions for the basis of activity selection when working with the mentally retarded. Also included are suggested instructional procedures that may facilitate teacher/student interaction in the learning process.

1. Minimize verbal explanation, and emphasize demonstration when presenting the activity.
2. Decide whether the activity is simple enough to be presented as a whole or whether it should be broken down into parts.
3. When introducing a new activity, it helps if everyone is seated preferably in a semicircle around the demonstrator.
4. Choose activities that are adaptable and flexible, and exclude or change activities that are beyond comprehension. These should either be eliminated or postponed until another session.
5. Short practice periods are usually best with frequent changes in activities.
6. The introduction of new activities should be presented early in the class session before fatigue, boredom, and attention become major factors that impede learning.
7. Vary the tempo (speed of activity) and excitement level throughout the activity period. One day a calm, slow activity may be used to start the class, building and climaxing to more stimulating activities, and ending with a noisy jumping activity, or vice versa.
8. Visual aids are extremely successful in explaining concepts.
9. Repetition, drill, and lots of review are necessary; however, be careful about boredom.

10. Challenge individuals and use different techniques to teach the same activity, e.g. problem solving as opposed to a command style teaching technique. Problem solving is beneficial because it brings past learning experiences together in order to solve a present problem. Command style teaching focuses on the teacher and presents the information directly to the mentally retarded participants.
11. Because many mentally retarded persons are good at imitating, the teacher should demonstrate activities only when absolutely necessary to allow for discovery.

Figure 6-3. Mentally retarded individuals should support and help each other whenever possible.

12. Respect age, and refrain from using activities that are inappropriate for the sexes, age, and type of disability.
13. Gain the group's attention before introducing an activity; make sure name tags are used if the participant's names are unknown, and limit the length of sessions to thirty minute periods initially, whenever possible.

Adapting Activities

Wheeler and Hooley (1969) have provided a guide for modifying activities so that they are adaptable to all participating individuals regardless of age, level, or handicap. This guide includes the following:

1. Shorten or vary distances required for throwing, running, etc., during a physical activity.
2. Use guide wires, handrails, and/or other devices for helping individuals to perform and meet potentials within each activity.
3. Change or modify the rules so that they do not contain as many limiting conditions that lessen success.
4. Allow two hands instead of one when accuracy or power are involved.
5. Any games requiring equipment such as baskets and/or nets at regulation heights or distances should be lowered and/or the distance changed appropriately.
6. Increase the size of the manipulative objective, striking implement, and/or projectile (ball) used in the activity, as well as the targets, whenever necessary.
7. Permit sitting positions to increase the stability in activities usually played in a standing position, when necessary.

CRITERIA FOR PROGRAM ASSESSMENT

Finally, it is the teacher's role to evaluate and assess the program to ascertain whether the goals were realized. The activities need to be reconsidered as to their effectiveness. Often it is difficult to assess improvement and progress within mentally retarded individuals for short periods of time; however, certain questions can be posed by the teacher of the mentally retarded for consideration.

1. Is the individual progressing physically, e.g. walk better, jump higher, and run faster, since starting the program?
2. Has coordination improved? Look for improved use of hands and reduced evidence of clumsiness and awkwardness.

3. Has the manipulation of the equipment been improved?
4. Is the individual less susceptible to fatigue? Can the same activity that was played four weeks ago now be continued for five to ten minutes longer?
5. Has strength increased, and is it in evidence more than before? (Is the individual capable of jumping higher or hitting a ball farther?)
6. Has body build (proportions) and weight overtly changed?

These questions will not provide the total evaluatory information needed for accurate assessment of the program, but they will help the teacher to recognize concrete levels of improvement that may help to depict the worthiness and effectiveness of the activities program in meeting the needs of the mentally retarded.

Individual Educational Plan (IEP) is an evaluative tool that may be valuable in the movement and rhythms program. The IEP is being used in schools throughout the United States for mentally retarded students and has been strongly advocated for physical education and recreation programs. A simplified and less intensive version of the IEP should be utilized and devised by the instructor if nothing else is readily available. Without evaluation, there is no concrete justification for the existence of the program.

Chapter 7

SUGGESTED PROGRAM ACTIVITIES AND EQUIPMENT

Emphasis has been placed, throughout the text, on selecting appropriate movement and rhythms activities that fit the needs of the mentally retarded population. The focus, therefore, has not been on what activity to select but rather on what prescribed activity would best benefit these needs of the participants, or on how an activity could be adapted to fit these needs. The movement and rhythms program can provide another approach in the educational process of the mentally retarded. Through orientation, exploration, dance, and/or rhythmic activities areas such as spacial orientation (environment), physical fitness, body awareness, and social skills may be developed. At the beginning of each movement and rhythm activity period, it is usually advisable to commence with a warm-up period to stimulate both the muscles and the interests of the participants. It is suggested that the teacher utilize the music and dance program within a recreational milieu as part of the education process of the mentally retarded. The following are suggested activities and equipment that have been used in a movement and rhythms program for the mentally retarded.

WARM-UP

As discussed previously, a warm-up period is necessary for preparing both the teacher and the mentally retarded for the movement and rhythms session. Suggested exercises that may help in the warm-up are the following:

1. Isolation exercises or exercises that warm up the fine motor muscles of the body. Such exercises might include the following:
   a. Squeezing a sponge ball in order to warm up the fingers and hands

b. Picking up a bean bag with the toes and dropping it into a pail
c. Blowing air into a balloon for respiratory and facial muscles
d. Using hula hoops to practice doing the hula around the waist, arms, legs, and neck areas of the body
e. Bouncing a basketball or smaller ball while remaining stationary, or walking around the room for warming the arms, upper torso, and lower torso

2. Gross motor exercises — involve large muscle groups of the body and should involve invigorating types of movement such as jumping and running. Suggested exercises are the following:
   a. Throwing a ball in various ways to a partner or among a group
   b. Rolling a ball in various ways to a partner or among a group
   c. Passing (two- or one-handed passing) the ball between partners
   d. Calisthenics such as jumping jacks, jogging, push-ups, and sit-ups
   e. Rope jumping individually or in groups

At the conclusion of the warm-up period, the participants should be ready to continue with the movement and rhythms program as it relates to areas of spacial orientation, physical fitness, body awareness, and social skills. The first area to be discussed is spacial orientation.

SPACIAL ORIENTATION

Spacial orientation is concerned primarily with movement that relates to spacial concepts, i.e. laterality, directionality, shapes, level, and design.

1. Laterality — deals with the concept of left- and right-sidedness. Equipment that can be used in these activities and that help in promoting this concept are the following:
   a. Hula hoops — rolled across the floor to a partner, first designating use of the right arm and later designating use of the left arm

    b. Singing dances — such as "Looby-loo" that give directions that stress laterality, recognition and recall

    c. Paper streamers — while moving to music around the room the dancers are instructed to hold the streamer in the left hand and then change to the right hand

    d. Lummi sticks — held in various positions utilize many right and left hand maneuvers

2. Directionality — is concerned with such movements through space as forward, backward, sideward, up, down, through, and around. Examples would be the following:

    a. Simon says game — instructions may be given for the participants to move forward, backward, etc.

    b. Giant steps — instructions would be provided that initiated various directions with counting, e.g. take two giant steps back

    c. "The Bus Song" — a singing activity that utilizes turning and up-down movements as dictated by the words in the song

    d. Balloon toss — between partners or groups is useful in teaching the concept of up and down

    e. Follow-the-leader — employs locomotion when individuals follow the selected leader around the room, over tables, under tables, and/or in between tables and chairs

3. Shapes and levels are primarily concerned with dimension, e.g. how large or small, thin or fat, high or low an object is. Such activities and equipment might include the following:

    a. Passing a large ball and small ball simultaneously among group members to increase object differentiation awareness (size)

    b. Passing a square bean bag and a round sponge ball among group members (shape)

    c. Using the game of horseshoes to point out the shape of the shoe as it relates to the vertical stake (curved versus straight)

    d. Rolling a basketball while seated on the floor, then rolling the basketball while standing (levels)

    e. Climbing a ladder, and then climbing a suspended

rope (size)

f. Cutting out large letters, e.g. a cardboard V and L, and forming the same letter with bodies (shape)

PHYSICAL FITNESS

As discussed in Chapter 2, physical fitness is an important part of the total program when working with the mentally retarded. Components such as muscular endurance, muscular strength, flexibility, power, speed, and agility are developed through the activities of running, skipping, and jumping during play.

1. Examples of physical fitness activities using a parachute would be the following:

a. Hamstring stretch — all participants are seated on the ground with their legs extended forward, backs straight, and their hands holding the edges of the para- chute tightly. The chute should be stretched but not taut. On the count of three, half of the participants, who are seated around one-half of the circle, will lie down, pulling the chute back toward their heads si- multaneously. This should force the other half of the group members in the circle to lean forward in order to continue holding onto the chute. If the members who are being pulled forward, lower their heads, stretch their arms, and keep their legs fully extended (not bent), a stretch will result under the backs of the legs or in the hamstring area. This exercise is repeated when the other half of the circle lies down on the ground, pulling forward the other half of the group.

b. Arm stretches — result when in the same seated posi- tion as described in a. The individuals should begin to travel backward (scooting) using their legs while main- taining hold of the chute with their hands and fingers. The farther back everyone in the circle moves, the tauter the parachute becomes, and the greater the stretch in the arms and shoulders is.

Exercises and activities that are conducive to strengthening muscles may also be part of a program using parachutes. Two examples of exercises that may increase muscular strength are the following:

c. Bent knee sit-ups — may increase strength in the abdominal muscles. The group should be seated on the ground holding onto the parachute with their fingers and hands; their knees should be bent with the bottoms of the feet touching the ground surface. Half of the group lower their backs to the ground while the other half remain sitting upright. This alternates back and forth so that half of the circle will be down and half up at all times. This exercise may be repeated approximately ten to twelve times, depending on the abilities of the group members.

d. Tug-of-war — used to develop back and shoulder strength and/or arms, legs, and chests. The entire group should be holding onto the parachute edges with their fingers and hands while facing in the direction *away* from the parachute. On the count of three, everyone begins to walk away from the parachute while maintaining hold of the chute. As the parachute begins to stretch tighter and tighter, the muscles in the arms and chest are forced to work harder. Intermittent periods of relaxation may be provided between the exercise sets of ten to twelve repetitions.

Muscular endurance activities require that an exercise be repeated more than ten to twelve times. Examples of muscular endurance activities are the following:

e. Shaking the parachute — continuously for approximately thirty to sixty seconds before resting. This activity is primarily for the fingers, hands, arms, and upper torso

f. Lifting the parachute — from a starting position on the ground to raising the parachute above head level, is good for working the legs, body, and arms

2. Bicycle inner tube pulls — encourages the participants to work on physical fitness individually or in groups. Suggested exercises might include the following:

a. Stretching the tire tube between the feet and arms while maintaining a standing position

   b. Stretching the tubes between the feet and arms while lying on the back

   c. Stretching the tire tubes between the arms, either in front of the chest or behind the chest

   d. Stretching the tube from an unusual body placement position, e.g. behind the neck and under the feet

   e. Stretching the tubes between the feet and arms and then jumping across the room

   f. Stretching the tubes as mentioned in a through e but in groups or partners

3. Tires — may also promote agility and power. By placing the tires in varied patterns across the floor, the participants can practice jumping in and out of the tires while moving (locomotor) across the room. For a challenge, the participants can be timed as they execute the obstacle course.

4. Stairs or benches — useful for developing strength and power, by running or jumping stairs or jumping on and off benches.

BODY AWARENESS

Activities that are designed to improve body part awareness or body control are a necessary program content for the mentally retarded. Inclusive within this area are activities that emphasize the following: (1) fine motor coordination, (2) gross motor coordination, (3) balance improvement, (4) eye-hand coordination, (5) eye-hand-foot coordination, and (6) sensory perception. Suggested activities include the following:

1. Chasing a balloon — while hitting it in the air would improve gross motor coordination

2. Pin the tail on the donkey — to promote kinesthetic awareness, sensory perception, and balance improvement

3. Throwing a scarf in the air — catching it for development of eye-hand coordination

4. Ping-Pong ball blow — used to promote breath control and fine motor coordination. On the hands and knees, the participants would attempt to blow the Ping-Pong ball across the floor.

5. Dribbling a balloon between the feet for several yards — targets eye-foot coordination
6. Running on the toes and walking a balance beam — focus on balance control
7. Drop-kicking a balloon — with stocking or bare feet would enhance development of eye-hand-foot coordination
8. Cymbals — clanging together or lummi sticks would enhance the development of eye-hand coordination and rhythm

As discussed previously, dance and music will probably play a fundamental role in the movement program for the mentally retarded. Through the executing of steps and basic dances; through singing, playing, and listening to music; and through combining dance, rhythms, and music activities, the mentally retarded may experience and explore movement. Dance activities are, therefore, a way in which the mentally retarded can recreate and have fun while developing an awareness of spacial orientation and improving physical fitness, body awareness, and social skills. Additional dance activities that help improve social skills, body awareness, physical fitness, and spacial orientation are delineated as follows. Certain basic dance props are also mentioned that may enhance the movement and rhythms program.

DANCE

Dance activities plus music can be a major force in controlling the mentally retarded's moods and feelings and for expressing attitudes and aggressions in socially acceptable ways. Calm movement accompanied by quiet and slow music may decrease the hyperactiveness of the excited member while participating. Loud rock music and quick abrupt movement may tend to excite and stimulate the somewhat withdrawn and lethargic participant. Whatever the purpose, dance is a means of bringing about desired reactions and movements within each mentally retarded person. Selected props, along with specifically chosen music, are a means of helping the dancer to concentrate fully and participate in the movement program. Props offer the dancer a vehicle in which moods and feelings can be transferred away from the confines of the body. This offers the individual a way to increase successful activity achievement. If an individual is requested to run across the room so that a scarf will be suspended into the air throughout the movement, the dancer can observe whether or not the scarf is truly suspended or hangs limply. The following is a list of suggested props and how they might be used in a movement program for the mentally retarded.

1. Scarves — help the dancer and the teacher to exemplify the energy being produced from the body and transferred through the arms, hands, and fingers to the scarf. The scarf should articulate as the arms are waved. As the body turns in a series of circular patterns, so should the scarf.
2. Ropes — a means of putting the body into twisted shapes and forms that are unusual. Group interaction can take place when ten or more participants take part in holding on to the rope and forming a human knot. As music is played, the group responds by moving around the room, between and around each other, twisting and turning until the music ends.
3. Balloons — useful because of their colors, texture, and sense of weightlessness. As music is played, the participants can practice responding appropriately to the musical accompaniment by moving around the room, tossing, bouncing, and/or blowing their balloons around in the air.
4. Hula hoops — beneficial in working with small groups or partners. They may be rolled, jumped in and out of, or used as props to be tossed. Like the scarf, hoops may be used to form an extension of the arm.
5. Other props and equipment — that may be beneficial to the movement and rhythms program for the mentally retarded might include the following:
   a. Shawls or ponchos — used to alter moods, or for fantasizing various character parts
   b. Hats — good for pretending and fantasizing (role playing)
   c. Various sized balls — extremely useful for dancers who are inhibited and require an object other than the *self*

to target
d. Beads or other sundry articles of clothing — promote role playing opportunities or promote themes for dances

Whenever one is working with the mentally retarded in a movement and rhythms program, it is helpful initially if the participants have become aware of and learned to react to specific cues given by the leader or teacher. This will help maintain control during the various activities and exercises, especially in situations where mass movement is taking place within the room. To restrict or impede bodies colliding into one another or to discipline the participants concerning when to move and when to stop cueing is effective. One particular activity that may help in teaching the participants the meaning of cues is Statues.

6. Statues — derived from the principle of freezing or posing. As the mentally retarded place themselves around the room, all stand still until the music begins. The music may be played fast or slow, quiet or loud. The objective is freezing when the music stops. In the beginning, the teacher can help by calling out "start" when the music begins and "stop" when the music stops. Other concepts such as directing the participants to change their levels from either high or low (spacial orientation) and to change the type of movement, e.g. jumping to skipping (physical fitness) is beneficial also.

Culminating the movement and rhythms session is just as important as warm-up. Relaxation activities are excellent for calming and winding down before departure. They may also be used throughout and/or at the beginning of the session, if deemed appropriate. The importance of a relaxation period is discussed next.

RELAXATION

At the conclusion, in the beginning, or at intermittent intervals it may be useful to provide relaxation activities. Relaxation activities may (1) quiet the individual, (2) provide increased awareness of the body (both internal and external), (3) help re-establish group control before leaving the session or before continuing to another activity, and (4) provide a time for reflection and evaluation of the session. Relaxation activities that may help when working with the mentally retarded are the following:

1. Begin by discussing the qualities and characteristics of an ice cream cone before and after it melts. Then the group can be directed to enact this experience.
2. The group can pretend to be rag dolls who fall down on the floor when completely limp.
3. At the end of a dance using scarves or shawls, the dancers can be instructed to lie quietly while covering their faces with the material.
4. At the end of a parachute activity, the participants can lift the parachute for one last time, and as the parachute drops down to the ground, the group members move under the chute and lie quietly.
5. The teacher can request the group to lie on the ground with eyes closed. Body parts, e.g. toes, ankles, legs, knees, and thighs, should be called out individually. The group is instructed to make these parts as light as possible so that they seem to become weightless. Relaxation of these body parts can be tested by the teacher by lightly shaking the area for tenseness. Although this activity is probably one of the best means of relaxing, it involves concentration and internal awareness of one's body. Therefore, it should not be expected that the group will begin to relax the body totally after only one day or even a couple of weeks using this method.

CONCLUSION

What are the necessary elements in a successful movement and rhythms program? How does one organize such a program? The teacher or leader must have the desire and motivation to seek knowledge, resources, and volunteers, when needed, to organize the program. Teachers trained in dance may have to seek special help from those who are familiar with the problems and characteristics of the mentally retarded population. Teachers who are not trained in dance but are used to working with the mentally retarded may need to rely on records of dance and music when organizing the program. It is through the knowledge, resources, and volunteers that the facility is provided; proper equipment may be found; props can be purchased, donated, or made; and assistants obtained. The movement and rhythms program does not have to be a *one man show* but rather a cooperative endeavor between the schools, community recreation centers, youth serving agencies (e.g. 4-H and scouts), parents, recreators, physical educators, dancers, musicians, school teachers, and any other interested volunteers.

The program may start as a special project between the schools and community at four-week intervals before extending into a weekly occurrence. Although the text does strongly suggest a progression format, it is better to whet appetites and instill program interest with small excerpts from the total program than to preclude any movement and rhythmic experience entirely.

The mentally retarded may also benefit from an integrated movement and rhythms program. The presence of nonretarded peers in an activity session may challenge and improve the mentally retarded's chances for achievement. Normalization of the mentally retarded will only result when the individuals are placed in a setting with nonretarded individuals. The key to a successful integrated program is in preparing the mentally retarded members and the nonmentally retarded members separately before they participate together. It is probably best to keep the two groups segregated initially and then to integrate occasionally at opportune times throughout the year.

The movement and rhythms program is a part of the whole creative arts movement that has been bourgeoning the last decade. Each child, whether handicapped or nonhandicapped "should be allowed to explore his talents and skills and learn to shape his thoughts and feelings into a form of artistic expression" (Sherrill and Cox, 1979). Movement orientation, exploration, dance, and rhythms provide approaches that will serve to meet the physical, psychological, and social needs of the mentally retarded through creative expression.

Figure 7-1. Mentally retarded and nonmentally retarded may be integrated in a special community dance project.

APPENDICES

1. The students will expose their senses to various tastes, smells, touches, sounds, and sights by
   a. tasting a lemon, honey, and salt;
   b. smelling alcohol, pine bark, and a flower;
   c. touching a piece of bark, shag carpet square, and a balloon;
   d. hearing sticks dropped on the floor, popcorn rattling in a can and creaking from the album *The Haunted House* — Disney Record; and
   e. sighting different colors that each individual is wearing, a dark closet, a glaring light bulb.
2. The students will practice running for one to three minutes without stopping.
3. The students will practice the following:
   a. crab walk
   b. bear walk
   c. seat walk
   d. leg straddles
4. Kinesthetic awareness — the students will work and practice manipulating body parts by doing the following:
   a. Trying to model the instructor as she places body parts in different positions (e.g. raises arm overhead).
   b. Working in pairs, one person who is blindfolded lies on the floor. The partner then moves a body part and returns it to the starting point.
   c. The blindfolded person must then reenact the identical movement.

RELAXATION/CONCLUSION: FIFTEEN MINUTES

1. Postural activities will help the students stand correctly aligned and improve overall movement efficiency by
   a. practice standing next to a wall placing shoulders, back of head, lower back, and back of the legs against the wall, and
   b. walking across the room balancing a bean bag on top of the head.
2. Lying in a supine position on the floor, the students should practice touching the floor with the lower back.
   a. The first time the knees should be bent.

EXAMPLES OF MOVEMENT AND MUSIC ACTIVITY LESSON PLANS FOR THE MENTALLY RETARDED

ACTIVITY 1

1.0 Goal (Movement Orientation)

Demonstrates abilities in the areas of physical fitness and perceptual-motor tasks.

1.1 Objectives

The student should be able to do the following:

1.11 identify at least fifteen different body parts (especially the primary sensory parts, e.g. ear, nose, eyes, mouth, fingers)
1.12 run for three minutes without stopping
1.13 perform muscular integration activities
1.14 perform flexibility and endurance exercises
1.15 perform two activities designed to improve posture

Tasks

WARM-UP: FIVE MINUTES
1. The song "Ob-la-di, Ob-la-da" (*Mod Marches*, Hap Palmer) will be played as the students march around the room. Scarves will be used to add variation and to increase movement possibilities with the marching.
2. The song "Foot to Head" (*Songs and Games of Physical Fitness for Boys and Girls*, Golden Records) will be used to sing and identify additional body parts.

SKILL DEVELOPMENT: TWENTY-FIVE MINUTES

one to three minutes without stopping
2. Exercises — the student will practice the following:
   a. crab walk, bear walk, butterfly, leg straddle, and seat walk
   b. hopping and jumping for a period of thirty to sixty seconds
   c. inner tube pull — two partners stand inside an inner tube and pull away from each other. May be done on the floor or standing.

SKILL APPLICATION: FIFTEEN MINUTES

1. Tinikling — the students will be introduced to the bamboo poles and the record *Elementary School Exercises to Music,* Hoctor and should
   a. listen to the tinikling music,
   b. clap to the tinikling music,
   c. hop to the tinikling music,
   d. jump to the music, and
   e. combine a hop and jump pattern to the music.
2. The students should work in pairs and
   a. practice the wheelbarrow exercise in which one partner holds the feet of the other partner, who is on the ground, and the two travel across the floor
   b. practice a three-legged walk and run with partners by tying the inside legs together

RELAXATION/CONCLUSION: TEN MINUTES

1. In partners, sitting on the floor, hold hands shoulder high and practice isometric exercising. Hands of the two partners should touch, both should use equal force and push against each other's hand for a five-second count.
2. In partners, on the floor, press backs together for five counts.
3. In partners, on the floor, press backs together and attempt to stand simultaneously and sit simultaneously. (Elbows of the partners should be hooked together.)
4. The final time should be spent lying on the floor, keeping the lower back in contact with the floor.

2.2 Materials Needed

1. Bamboo poles
2. Record player/records

b. The second time the legs should be completely extended.

1.2 Materials Needed

1. Records and record player
2. Bean bags (15)
3. Lemons, salt, honey, pine bark, flowers, alcohol, carpet squares, balloons, lummi sticks, popcorn in a can
4. Stop watch
5. Blindfolds

ACTIVITY 2

2.0 Goal (Movement Orientation)

Demonstrates abilities in the area of physical fitness and perceptual-motor tasks.

2.1 Objectives

The student should be able to do the following:

2.11 identify at least fifteen body parts
2.12 run for three minutes without stopping
2.13 perform muscular integration activities (i.e. tinikling)
2.14 perform various flexibility and endurance exercises with a partner
2.15 perform two activities designed to improve posture

Tasks

WARM-UP: FIVE MINUTES
1. Marching — to the song "Happy Together" (*Mod Marches*, Hap Palmer)
2. Shake and wiggle — to the album *26 All Purpose Action Tunes* the instructor will lead the students in shaking and wiggling various body parts

SKILL DEVELOPMENT: FIFTEEN MINUTES
1. Running — the students will attempt to run in place for

each end, are needed to manipulate the poles. The rhythm must be kept steady and not increased or slowed once started.

2. The students should practice jumping between and away from two chalk drawn lines used to represent the poles, before trying to jump the poles. If successful, try it with the poles.

3. Everyone should at least try jumping the chalk lines (two times between the lines and one time out) and tapping out the rhythm while manipulating the poles.

RELAXATION/CONCLUSION: FIVE MINUTES

The students should practice maintaining their lower backs on the floor while lying on the floor.

3.2 Materials Needed

1. Record player/records
2. Bamboo poles
3. Stopwatch
4. Chalk

ACTIVITY 4

4.0 Goal (Movement Exploration)

Demonstrates abilities in the areas of locomotor/nonlocomotor and movement component/quality tasks.

4.1 Objectives

The student should be able to do the following:

    4.11 perform five locomotor tasks.
    4.12 perform five nonlocomotor tasks.
    4.13 demonstrate five movement components
    4.14 demonstrate two movement qualities.

Tasks

WARM-UP: FIVE MINUTES
The students will review the songs as follow:

3. Inner tubes
4. Scarves
5. Stop watch

ACTIVITY 3

3.0 Goal (Movement Orientation)

Demonstrates abilities in the areas of physical fitness and perceptual motor tasks.

3.1 Objectives

The student should be able to do the following:

3.11 identify at least fifteen different body parts
3.12 run for two minutes without stopping
3.13 perform a tinikling dance
3.14 perform flexibility, endurance, and posture exercises
3.15 work in pairs or groups

Tasks

WARM-UP: FIFTEEN MINUTES
1. The following body identification songs learned during the last two weeks will be reviewed:
   a. "Make Your Eyes" and "Hands Go Up and Down" (*Everyday Skills*, Kimbo).
   b. "Foot to Head" (*Songs and Games of Physical Fitness for Boys and Girls*, Golden Records).
2. Marching to music from the album *Mod Marches*, Hap Palmer.

SKILL DEVELOPMENT: FIFTEEN MINUTES
1. Review the tinikling song from the album *Elementary School Exercises to Music*, Hoctor.
2. Practice hopping and jumping to the music.
3. Practice running for one to three minutes without stopping.

SKILL APPLICATION: TWENTY MINUTES
1. Practice manipulating the tinikling sticks to a three count, down-down-together, pattern. Two students, one at

The teacher tells the story of how the carpet flies, what the carpet flies over or by, what are events taking place on earth, and how the carpet is landing. Quiet music is played in the background, and the room should be darkened.

4.2 Materials Needed

1. Record player/records
2. Carpet squares
3. Drum

ACTIVITY 5

5.0 Goal (Dance Foundation)

Demonstrates abilities in the areas of basic dance skills, and terminology tasks.

5.1 Objectives

The student should be able to do the following:

5.11 demonstrate one basic dance step.
5.12 perform two locomotor steps combined with a movement component and movement quality.
5.13 perform a creative dance (specifically Jack and Jill).
5.14 recognize and identify several terms/positions that are associated with dance, e.g. relevé, plié, arabesque, and lunge.

Tasks

WARM-UP: FIVE MINUTES

1. The song "I Like to Dance" (*Everyday Skills*, Kimbo) will be introduced and practiced.
2. The song will be repeated and practiced again.
3. The song will be repeated as the students work with a partner.

a. "Make Your Eyes" and "Hands Go Up and Down" (*Everyday Skills*, Kimbo).

b. "Foot to Head" (*Songs and Games of Physical Fitness for Boys and Girls*, Golden Records).

SKILL DEVELOPMENT: FIFTEEN MINUTES

1. The following locomotor steps will be reviewed and practiced:
   a. hop
   b. jump
   c. walk
   d. run
   e. leap
   f. step hop
2. The gallop and skip will be introduced.
3. The walk and run will be used to change space, levels, focus, direction, and gesture as the students move around the room.
4. The qualities of percussive and sustained movement will be introduced during the walk/run movement.

APPLICATION OF SKILLS: FIFTEEN MINUTES

1. Magic carpet ride — each student is given a carpet square and told to sit on the square. The magic carpet ride should follow the following sequences:
   a. The students discuss with the teacher different movements that can occur without ever moving the body away from the carpet (e.g. twisting, bending, swinging, and collapsing).
   b. The students listen to the music "1001 Nights", *Ferrante and Teicher* to sense the mood and to become familiar with the tempo, melody, and phrasing of the piece.
   c. The students and teacher discuss what images result when listening to the music (e.g. a blue sky, mountains, rivers, plains).
   d. The students practice their movements to the music.

CONCLUSION/RELAXATION: TEN MINUTES

1. The students practice the leap, gallop, and skip to a drum beat.
2. The students lie on their carpet squares with eyes closed.

3. The students will be shown pictures of four professional dancers in these poses.

5.2 Materials Needed

1. Record player/records
2. Chart
3. Cards of different dance positions
4. Drum
5. Pictures of dancers

ACTIVITY 6

6.0 Goal (Dance Foundation)

Demonstrates abilities in the areas of basic dance skills and terminology tasks.

6.1 Objectives

The students should be able to do the following:

6.11 demonstrate one basic dance step.
6.12 perform at least one movement step.
6.13 demonstrate ability to compose and improvisational dance (nonlocomotor)
6.14 recognize and identify the plié, relevé, arabesque, and lunge from pictures.

Tasks

WARM-UP: FIVE MINUTES
1. The "Hora" will be played. The students should attempt to move continuously for 1.5 minutes.
2. The song "I Like to Dance" (*Everyday Skills*, Kimbo) will be performed.

SKILL DEVELOPMENT: FIFTEEN MINUTES
1. The hop, skip, gallop, slide, schottische, and two-step will be practiced
   a. individually;
   b. in pairs; and

SKILL DEVELOPMENT: FIFTEEN MINUTES

1. The students will review the walk, hop, jump, leap, skip, gallop, and slide to a drum beat.
2. The students will practice the steps holding the hand of a partner.
3. The students will practice the walk, hop, and jump individually, but they will add the turning concept. They will practice a turning walk, turning hop, and a turning jump.
4. The students will be introduced to the schottische (step-together-step-hop in 4/4 time).

SKILL APPLICATION: FIFTEEN MINUTES

1. The students will work in pairs and practice performing the schottische in front of the other partner. They should take turns helping one another with the dance step.
2. The students will practice the schottische to a drum beat and to the "Texas Bummel Schottische" song (*Folk Dance Music*).
3. The students will review and practice the dance steps taught to the "La Raspa."
4. The instrumental "Jack and Jill" will be played as the students
   a. listen and sing the words listed on a chart;
   b. discuss the different movements that could be applied to the verses (e.g. tumbling, fetch, went up the hill, and fell down);
   c. practice the movements while reciting the verse; and
   d. practice the movements with the music.

   There is no right or wrong movement, only appropriate. Students should therefore start from any position they want (floor, standing) and depict the key movements creatively and individually.

RELAXATION/CONCLUSION: TEN MINUTES

1. The students will be shown pictures of different dance performers, e.g. folk dancers, ballet dancers, modern dancers, tap dancers, square dancers, jazz dancers, and child dancers.
2. The students will be shown the words relevé, plié, lunge, and arabesque. These will be demonstrated by posing four students.

and terminology tasks.

7.1 Objectives

The student should be able to do the following:

7.11 demonstrate two basic dance steps
7.12 recognize and identify several terms/positions that are associated with dance
7.13 perform a creative dance (popcorn)
7.14 perform a simple dance (Old Brass Wagon)

Tasks

WARM-UP: FIVE MINUTES
Students choose.

SKILL DEVELOPMENT: FIFTEEN MINUTES
1. The students will practice the walk, turn, hop, and slide as follows:
   a. individually
   b. in a circle
2. The elbow swing and shuffle will be introduced individually and in a circle.
3. The movement components and qualities will be reviewed.

SKILL APPLICATION: TWENTY MINUTES
1. The song "Old Brass Wagon" will be sung. The students will do the following:
   a. practice singing the words
   b. practice the steps that correspond to the verses, e.g. "Circle to Right, Old Brass Wagon"
   c. practice the steps and song as individuals
2. The popcorn dance will be performed. The students will do the following:
   a. discuss the sequence involved in corn popping
   b. discuss the movement qualities and movement components that *may* be appropriate
   c. find a starting point in the room
   d. listen to the song "Popcorn" (*Wake Up Calm Down,*

c. in a circle accompanied by music.
2. The movement components and qualities will be reviewed.

SKILL APPLICATION: TWENTY MINUTES

1. Follow the leader — will be accompanied by music from *Activities for Individualization*, Activity Records. The students will do the following:
   a. select a basic step (jump, hop, etc.) or dance step (schottische, two-step, etc.)
   b. practice the step
   c. take turns leading the rest of the group performing the step
2. The students will sit on a carpet square and do the following:
   a. listen to the music "Manhattan Rhapsody"
   b. discuss possible nonlocomotor movements that might be performed
   c. practice the dance
   d. add possible movement components and qualities if necessary
   e. use scarves to perform the nonlocomotor dance again

RELAXATION/CONCLUSION: FIVE MINUTES

1. Identify the plié, relevé, lunge, arabesque, walk, and pirouette pictures.
2. Review the relaxation technique imitating an ice cream cone slowly melting.

6.2 Materials Needed

1. Record player/record
2. Pictures
3. Scarves
4. Carpet squares

ACTIVITY 7

7.0 Goal (Dance Foundation)

Demonstrates abilities in the areas of basic dance skills

leap, slide as follows:

    a. individually

    b. in partners

    c. in a circle

2. The students will practice the schottische, two-step, and polka individually.

3. The students will review the tinikling exercise taught previously practicing with chalk drawn lines substituting as poles.

SKILL APPLICATION: FIFTEEN MINUTES

1. The students will listen to the song "Clapping Hands, Walking" (*Rhythms*, Honor Your Partner).

    a. the students will clap with the music

    b. the students will walk around the room to the music

    c. the students will walk and clap to the music

    d. the students may choose whether to try hopping, jumping, or leaping to the music

2. The students will use the jump, hop, and leap in the tinikling dance. Two volunteers will be needed to manipulate the bamboo poles:

    a. a 3/4 time will be used of down-down-together.

    b. clap the rhythm first.

    c. the students will jump twice between the poles and once outside.

    d. walking between the poles may be necessary if jumping is too difficult.

CONCLUSION/RELAXATION: FIVE MINUTES

Free choice of singing activities.

8.2 Materials Needed

1. Record player/records
2. Chalk
3. Tinikling poles

ACTIVITY 9

9.1 Goal (Rhythms)

Demonstrates abilities in the area of rhythm tasks.

Educational Activities)
e. perform to the song
CONCLUSION/RELAXATION: FIVE MINUTES
The students will be served popcorn and discuss the movement that took place during the dance.

7.2 Materials Needed

1. Record player/records
2. Popcorn

ACTIVITY 8

8.0 Goal (Rhythms)

Demonstrates abilities in the area of rhythm tasks.

8.1 Objectives

The student should be able to do the following:

8.11 perform one action song
8.12 perform two basic movement steps and one dance step
8.13 perform a rhythms exercise routine
8.14 perform a rhythm dance (tinikling).

Tasks

WARM-UP: TEN MINUTES
1. The students will be introduced to the song "If You're Happy and You Know it Clap Your Hands." The student shall practice the following:
   a. clap hands
   b. stamp feet
   c. nod your head
   d. do all three
2. The students will review the dance "Old Brass Wagon."
SKILL DEVELOPMENT: FIFTEEN MINUTES
1. The students will practice the hop, skip, jump, gallop,

f. tap elbows with arms crossed
3. The students will help devise a lummi stick routine combining the above steps. The teacher will chart the routine.
4. The students will then perform the routine to *And the Beat Goes on,* Education Activities and Kimbo.

CONCLUSION/RELAXATION: TEN MINUTES

The students will be exposed to tap dancing. A dancer will exhibit certain basic steps and easy time steps for the students.

9.2 Materials Needed

1. Record player/records
2. Lummi sticks
3. Chart and pen

ACTIVITY 10

10.0 Goal (Dance)

Demonstrate abilities in the area of square dance.

10.1 Objectives

The student should be able to do the following:

10.11 perform a dance with a partner
10.12 perform a dance in a group of four
10.13 perform two square dance steps
10.14 perform a square dance

Tasks

WARM-UP: FIVE MINUTES

1. Review marching and clapping to *Patriotic Morning Time Songs.*
2. Simon says — students take turns being Simon.

SKILL DEVELOPMENT: FIFTEEN MINUTES

1. Review the schottische, polka, two-step, and mazurka.
2. Review the following terms:
   a. honor your partner

9.1 Objectives

The student should be able to do the following:

9.11 perform one action song.

9.12 perform two basic movement steps and one dance step.

9.13 perform a rhythms exercise routine.

9.14 manipulate lummi sticks, coordinating right hand with left hand in different positions.

Tasks

WARM-UP: FIVE MINUTES

1. Introduce the song "One Finger One Thumb."
2. Review the song "If You're Happy."
3. Practice the hop, skip, and leap to a drum beat.

SKILL DEVELOPMENT: TEN MINUTES

1. The students will practice the schottische, two-step, and polka holding hands with a partner and individually.
2. The students will sit on the floor and practice the following:
   a. clapping — overhead, sides
   b. tapping — shoulders, head, thighs
   c. tapping the floor — front, side, back
   d. slapping — knees

SKILL APPLICATION: FIFTEEN MINUTES

1. The students will be given one lummi stick and do the following:
   a. tap the floor — front, side, back
   b. shoulder
   c. hand
   d. neighbors stick
2. The students will manipulate two lummi sticks as follows:
   a. tap floor — front, side, both sides, simultaneously, back
   b. tap shoulders
   c. tap sticks
   d. rub sticks together
   e. tap knees

Appendix B

TABLE 1

EVEN AND UNEVEN RHYTHMIC PATTERNS FOR EIGHT BASIC STEPS IN A MOVEMENT PROGRAM

Time Signature		Rhythmic Pattern	Locomotor Movement	Description
4/4	even		walk	a series of steps on alternate feet resulting from the losing and regaining of equilibrium
2/2	even		run	a series of quick, successive steps – only one foot should be touching the ground
4/4	even		jump	lift up into the air and land on two feet
4/4	even		hop	lift up in the air on one foot and land on same foot
4/4	even		leap	transfer to weight from one foot to the other with elevation between transfers
4/4	uneven		skip	step-hop combination repeated in a series
4/4	uneven		slide	gliding step in which one foot maintains contact with the ground
6/8	uneven		gallop	cutting step where Rf takes the place of the Lf or vice versa

114

  b. star
  c. do-si-do
  d. shuffle step
  e. allemande right and left
3. Introduce the following terms:
  a. pass-through
  b. grand right and left
  c. promenade
4. Practice the square dance steps, individually, with partners, and in groups of four.

SKILL APPLICATION: FIFTEEN MINUTES
  1. Review the Virginia reel by practicing the steps.
  2. Practice the steps with a partner.
  3. Perform the Virginia reel.
  4. Review the song and dance "Old Brass Wagon."

CONCLUSION/RELAXATION: TEN MINUTES
  1. Discussion on square dance with pictures as follow:
    a. purpose
    b. callers
    c. costume
  2. Practice lower back exercises.

10.2 Materials needed

  1. Record player/records

TABLE 3

MOVEMENT CHECKLIST

Body Part Identification	*Occurrence*	*Nonoccurrence*
A. Appendages		
1. arms	_____	_____
2. elbows	_____	_____
3. legs	_____	_____
4. knees	_____	_____
5. hands	_____	_____
6. feet	_____	_____
7. fingers	_____	_____
8. toes	_____	_____
B. Head		
1. eyebrows	_____	_____
2. ears	_____	_____
3. mouth	_____	_____
4. cheeks	_____	_____
5. eyes	_____	_____
6. forehead	_____	_____
7. chin	_____	_____
C. Upper Torso		
1. shoulders	_____	_____
2. stomach	_____	_____
3. back	_____	_____
4. shoulder blades	_____	_____
5. neck	_____	_____
6. ribs	_____	_____
D. Lower Torso		
1. pelvis	_____	_____
2. seat	_____	_____
3. hips	_____	_____
4. waist	_____	_____
5. thighs	_____	_____

E. Combined-request identification of two parts simultaneously
    1. upper torso

TABLE 2

EVEN AND UNEVEN RHYTHMIC PATTERNS FOR
FIVE BASIC DANCE STEPS

Dance Step	Uneven	Even	Time	Description
schottische	*(musical notation)*	*(musical notation)*	4/4	step-close-step-hop
polka	*(musical notation)* or *(musical notation)*		2/4	step-close-step-hop
two-step	*(musical notation)*		2/4	step-close-step-pause
mazurka		*(musical notation)*	3/4	leap-stamp-step
waltz		*(musical notation)*	3/4	step-close-step

TABLE 4

MOVEMENT REPERTOIRE ASSESSMENT

Rudimentary Mechanics of Movement	*Unskilled*	*Skilled*
able to bend the knees on command	_____	_____
able to rise on the toes on command	_____	_____
bends the upper body-forward, sideward, backward	_____	_____
lifts the lower body-lying on the floor	_____	_____
lifts legs forward, sideward, backward	_____	_____
demonstrates the following:		
lift	_____	_____
grasp	_____	_____
pull	_____	_____
over	_____	_____
under	_____	_____
around	_____	_____
inside	_____	_____
outside	_____	_____
beside	_____	_____
locomotion		
walk	_____	_____
run	_____	_____
jump	_____	_____
hop	_____	_____
leap	_____	_____
gallop	_____	_____
slide	_____	_____
skip	_____	_____
nonlocomotion		
collapse	_____	_____
swing	_____	_____
bend	_____	_____
twisting	_____	_____
stamping	_____	_____

Directional information as it relates to shape, space, and other objects

a. arms
b. head
c. waist   _____   _____
2. upper/lower torso
    a. arms
    b. legs   _____   _____

The evaluator questions the mentally retarded on body part identification by asking the individual to identify the following anatomical parts. Replies by the individual should be provided by touching each part.

34. *Singing Games for Little People* — Kimbo KIM 0880
35. *Activities for Individualization in Movement and Music* — Educational Activities AR 49
36. *Special Music for Special People* — Educational Activities AR 85
37. *Easy Does It: Activity Songs for Basic Motor Skill Development* — Hap Palmer — Educational Activities AR 581
38. *Get Ready to Square Dance* — Educational Activities AR 68
39. *The Feel of Music* — Hap Palmer — Educational Activities AR 556
40. *Wake Up! Calm Down through Rhythm and Dance* — Vol. II — Educational Activities AR 699
41. *Patriotic and Morning Time Songs* — Educational Activities AR 519
42. *Mod Marches* — Educational Activities AR 527
43. *Finger Games* — Educational Activities LP 506
44. *Classroom Records* — Fundamental Kimbo LP 3090
45. *Developing Everyday Day Skills through Movement and Songs* — Kimbo LP 7019
46. *Songs and Games of Physical Fitness for Boys and Girls* — Golden Records LP 114
47. *Elementary School Exercises to Music* — Hoctor Dance Records HLP 4008
48. *26 All Purpose Action Tunes* — Hoctor Dance Records HLP 4068/69

SUGGESTED RECORDS FOR THE MOVEMENT AND RHYTHMS PROGRAM

1. *Folk Dances from Round the World* — Vols. I-V Series I DRCC 601
2. *Folk Dances from Many Lands* — Rhythms Productions CC 607
3. *Folk Dances of North America* — Rhythms Productions CC 608
4. *Debka — Israeli Folk Dances* — Tikv DRLP TK 24
5. *Folk Dances of the World* — Hector HLP 4003
6. *Folk Dancing for High School and College Level* — Hector HLP 4029
7. *Modern Dance* — Bruce King KLP 4010
8. *Music for Modern Dance Technique* — Betram Ross/Edward Muller DRLP 4086/4087/4088
9. *Singing Square Dance* — Albums 1-8 — Bowmar B213-5/232
10. *Big Circle Mountain Square Dancing* — (2 copies) Educational Activities AR 52
11. *Square Dances Album 2* — Educational Activities HYR 2
12. *Modern Square Dancing* — Vol. 1 and 2 with calls, Vol. 2 without calls — Kimbo LP 4060, 5080
13. *Promenade and Do-Si-Do* — Educational Recordings SO 2
14. *And the Beat Goes On* — Kimbo LP 5020
15. *And the Beatles Go On and On* — Kimbo OP 8090
16. *Parachute Activities with Folk Dance Music* — Kimbo LP 9090
17. *Rhythmic Parachute Play* — Kimbo LP 6020
18. *Musical Ball Skills* — Activity Records Album 30
19. *Ball Gymnastics* — Kimbo 4030
20. *Getting to Know Myself* — Hap Palmer — Educational Activities AR 543
21. *To Move Is to Be* — Jo Ann Seker — Educational Activities LP 8060
22. *Movement Exploration* — Educational Activities — Kimbo LP 5090
23. *Fun Activities for Perceptual Motor Skills* — Kimbo KIM 9071
24. *Basic Popular Music* — Educational Activities LP 509
25. *Lummi Stick Fun* — Kimbo LP 2000
26. *Tinikling* — Carmencita Y. Kazar — Kimbo LP 9015
27. *Contemporary Tinikling Activities* — Boyd Pextor KEA 3095
28. *Soul Folk Dances* — Educational Activities AR 573
29. *Authentic Indian Dances and Folklore* — Kimbo LP 9070
30. *Around the World in Dance* — Educational Activities AR 542
31. *Folk Dances for Children* — Hector Records HLP 4001
32. *Honor Your Partner* — Educational Activities #20
33. *Honor Your Partner* — Educational Activities #10

119

London: MacDonald and Evans, 1975.

Lockhart, Aileene and Pease, Esther E. *Modern Dance*, 4th ed. Dubuque, IA: William C. Brown Co., Pubs., 1973.

Merrill, Toni. *Activities for the Aged and Infirm*. Springfield: Charles C Thomas, Publisher, 1967.

Mississippi School Bulletin No. 165 — *A Handbook on the Theory and Practice of Music for Educable Mentally Retarded Children and Youth*. Division of Instruction. State Dept. of Education, Jackson, MS. June, 1968.

Moran, Joan, and Kalakian, Leonard H. *Movement Experiences for the Mentally Retarded or Emotionally Disturbed Child*. Minneapolis, MN: Burgess Publishing Co., 1974.

Mosston, Muska. *Development Movement*. Columbus, OH: Charles E. Merrill Publishing Co., 1965.

Murdoch, Elizabeth B. *Expressive Movement*. London: W and R Chambers, 1973.

Murray, Ruth Lovell. *Dance in Elementary Education*, 3rd ed. New York: Harper & Row Pubs., Inc., 1975.

Nelson, Esther L. *Movement Games for Children of All Ages*. New York: Sterling Publishing Co., Inc., 1976.

Nordoff, Paul and Robbins, Clive. *Music Therapy in Special Education*. New York: John Day Co., Inc., 1971.

Physical Activities for the Mentally Retarded: Ideas for Instruction. Project on Recreation and Fitness for the Mentally Retarded and Lifetime Sports Education. Project of the American Association for Health, Physical Education and Recreation. 1201-165th St. N.W., Washington, D. C., 1968.

Physical Activities for Mentally Retarded Adults and Children. Report of Virginia's Seminars on Physical Activities for the Mentally Retarded. Published by the Virginia Mental Retardation Planning Council. The Division of State Planning and Community Affairs. Governor's Office, Office of Administration, Commonwealth of Virginia, 1010 James Madison Building, Richmond, Va., 1968.

Purvis, Jennie and Samet, Shelly. *Music in Developmental Therapy*. Baltimore: University Park Press, 1976.

Raebeck, Lois and Wheeler, Lawrence. *New Approaches to Music in the Elementary School*, 2nd ed. Dubuque, IA: William C. Brown Co., Pubs., 1970.

Recreation and Physical Activity for the Mentally Retarded. Council for Exceptional Children and American Association for Health, Physical Education and Recreation. 1201 Sixteenth Street, Washington, D. C., 1966.

Redfern, H. Bett. *Introducing Laban Art of Movement*. London: MacDonald and Evans, 1965.

Robins, Ferris and Robins, Janet. *Educational Rhythmics for Mentally Handicapped Children*. New York: Horizon Press Pubs., 1965.

Robinson, Christopher M., Harrison, Julie and Gridley, Joseph, *Physical*

BIBLIOGRAPHY

American Dance Therapy Association. *Proceedings of the Eighth Annual Conference American Dance Therapy Association,* Overland Park, Kansas, October 18-21, 1973.

Antey, John W. *Sing and Learn.* New York: John Day Co., Inc., 1965.

Bergethon, Bjornar and Boardman, Eunice. *Musical Growth in the Elementary School,* 3rd ed. New York: Holt, Rinehart & Winston, 1975.

Bryant, Rosalie and Oliver, Eloise McLean. *Fun and Fitness Through Elementary Physical Education.* West Nyack, New York: Parker Publishing Co., Inc., 1967.

Corbin, Charles B. *Inexpensive Equipment for Games, Play, and Physical Activity.* Dubuque, IA: William C. Brown, Co., Pubs., 1973.

Cratty, Bryant J. *Motor Activity and the Education of Retardates.* Philadelphia: Lea and Febiger, 1969.

Crews, Katherine. *Music and Perceptual-Motor Development.* Classroom Music Enrichment Units. New York: The Center for Applied Research in Education, Inc., 1975.

Doll, Edna and Nelson, Mary Jane. *Rhythms Today.* Morristown, NJ: Silver Burdett Co., 1965.

Driver, Ann. *Music and Movement.* London: Oxford University Press, 1970.

Ginglend, David R. and Stiles, Winifred E. *Music Activities for Retarded Children: A Handbook for Teachers and Parents.* Nashville, TN: Abingdon Press, 1965.

Godfrey, Barbara B. and Kephart, Newell C. *Movement Patterns and Motor Education.* Englewood Cliffs, NJ: Prentice-Hall, Inc., 1969.

Harris, Jane A., Pittman, Anne and Waller, Marlys S. *Dance A While: Handbook of Folk, Square, and Social Dance,* 5th ed., Minneapolis, MN: Burgess Publishing Co., 1978.

Hood, Marguerite V., and Schultz E.J. *Learning Music Through Rhythm.* Westport, CT: Greenwood Press, Inc., 1972.

Humphrey, Doris. *The Art of Making Dances.* New York: Grove Press, Inc., 1959.

Jaques-Dalcroze, Emile. *Eurhythmics, Art and Education.* Translated by Frederick Rothwell, 1972. New York: Arno Press, 1930.

Jaques-Dalcroze, Emile. *Rhythm, Music and Education.* Translated by Harold F. Rubinsteing, 1976. New York: Arno Press, 1921.

Jensen, Clayne R. and Jensen, Mary. *Square Dancing.* Provo, UT: Brigham Young University Press, 1973.

Laban, Rudolf. *Modern Education Dance,* 3rd ed. Revised by Lisa Ullmann.

Activity in the Education of Slow-Learning Children. London: Edward Arnold Publ., 1970.

Schlotter, Bertha E. and Svendsen, Margaret. *An Experiment in Recreation with the Mentally Retarded.* State of Illinois, The Illinois Institute for Juvenile Research, 1951.

Schurr, Evelyn L. *Movement Experiences for Children: Curriculum and Methods for Elementary School Physical Education.* New York: Appleton-Century-Crofts, Educational Division, Meredith Corp., 1967.

Sherrill, Claudine and Cox, Rosann. Personnel preparation in creative arts for the handicapped: Implications for improving the quality of Life. *Creative Arts for the Severely Handicapped.* Edited by Claudine Sherril. Springfield: Charles C Thomas, Publisher, 1979.

Swanson, Bessie R. *Music in the Education of Children,* 3rd ed. Belmont, CA: Wadsworth Publishing Co., Inc., 1969.

Thronton, Samuel. *Laban's Theory of Movement: A New Perspective.* Boston: Plays, Inc., 1971.

Wallis, Earl L. and Logan, Gene A. *Exercise for Children.* Englewood Cliffs, NJ: Prentice-Hall, Inc., 1966.

Werner, Peter H. and Simons, Richard A. *Inexpensive Physical Education Equipment for Children.* Minneapolis, MN: Burgess Publishing Co., 1976.

What is Dance Therapy Really? Proceedings of the Seventh Annual Conference American Dance Therapy Association, Santa Monica, CA, October 19-23, 1972.

Wheeler, Ruth H. and Hooley, Agnes M. *Physical Education for the Handicapped.* Philadelphia: Lea and Febiger, 1969.

Wickstrom, Ralph L. *Fundamental Motor Patterns.* Philadelphia: Lea and Febiger, 1970.

Winters, Shirley J. *Creative Rhythmic Movement For Children of Elementary School Age.* Dubuque, IA: William C. Brown Co., Pubs., 1975.

run, 35
skip, 36
slide, 36
turn, 36
walk, 34
Lummi activities, 67-68, 72

M

Mentally retarded, 6-8
Movement, 4
  locomotor, 31, 34-36
  movement analysis, 49
  movement components, 31, 37-38
  movement qualities, 31, 38-40
  music, 7
  nonlocomotor, 31-34

N

Normalization, 93
Noverre, Jean Georges, 41

P

Parachute activities, 41, 63, 72
Perceptual motor activities, 9-17, 29
  balance (*see* Balance)
  muscular integration, 9, 15-18, 24, 29, 87
  sensory motor, 8, 10-11, 25, 29, 76, 87
Physical fitness, 9, 24-29, 85
  cardiorespiratory endurance, 24, 26-27
  endurance, 24, 27-28, 30, 42, 85
  flexibility, 24, 26, 85

muscular strength, 24-26, 42, 85
Posture, 28-29
Programming, 4, 74, 78
  activity objectives, 77-78
  assessment, 80
  pupil objectives, 75-77
  teacher objectives, 74-75

R

Relaxation, 90-91
Rhythm, 5-6, 60, 72
  broken rhythm, 60
  continuous rhythm, 60
Rhythmic activities, 66, 72
Rhythm instruments, 62-63, 72

S

Schllotter, Bertha E. and Svendson, Margaret, 74
Sherrill, Claudine and Cox, Rosann, 93

T

Tinikling activities, 17, 68
Tumbling, 9, 18-24, 29

W

Warm-up, 82-83
Wheeler, Ruth H. and Hooley, Agnes M., 80

INDEX

A

Action songs, 60-61
Adapting activities, 78, 80

B

Balance, 11-15, 87
 dynamic balance, 11, 13-15
 static balance, 11-13
Ball activities, 16, 69-70, 72
Body awareness, 4-5, 8, 87-88
Bryant, Rosalie and McLean, Oliver, 67

C

Choreography (elements of)
 design, 37, 83
 direction, 37, 38
 focus, 38
 gesture, 37, 38
 level, 37, 83
 shape, 26, 37, 83-85
 space, 37
Chinese rope activities, 69
Circle dances, 65
Clapping activities, 70-71
Coordination, 42, 87
Cratty, Bryant, 4

D

Dance, 41, 88 (Specific steps)
 Mazurka, 38
 Polka, 38
 Schottische, 37
 Two-step, 38
 Waltz, 39
Dance forms
 creative dance, 54-58
 folk dance, 42-44, 58
 modern dance, 47-54, 58
 square dance, 44-47, 58
Dancer, 41
Dancing, 41, 50
Dance Therapy (*Focus on Dance VII*), 4
Directionality, 83, 84

E

Evaluation, 80-81

G

Godfrey, Barbara B. and Kephart, Newell
 C., 4

H

Humphrey, Doris, 59

I

Individualized Education Plan, 81
Integration, 93

J

Jaques-Dalcroze, Emile, 5, 6
Jumprope activities, 17, 70, 72

K

Kinesthesis, 5, 8, 29

L

Laban, Rudolf, 41
Laterality, 40, 83-84
Locomotor activities (basic)
 gallop, 36
 hop, 35
 jump, 35
 leap, 35